MUSINGS

2014-2015

David Neill

INTRODUCTION

The *Musings* blog continues though the subject matter is more varied. Movie reviews are much more frequent, though politics is still the main subject of the blog. The rise of Trump is discussed in the latter half of 2015 (thus reprinting blogs I compiled in *Blogging Trump*).

2014

Welcome to the Ice Age

Frozen Out: 98% of Stories Ignore That Ice-bound Ship Was On Global Warming Mission

A group of climate change scientists were rescued by helicopter Jan. 2, after being stranded in the ice since Christmas morning. But the majority of the broadcast networks' reports about the ice-locked climate researchers never mentioned climate change.

The Russian ship, Akademic Shokalskiy, was stranded in the ice while on a climate change research expedition, yet nearly 98 percent of network news reports about the stranded researchers failed to mention their mission at all. Forty out of 41 stories (97.5 percent) on the network morning and evening news shows since Dec. 25 failed to mention climate change had anything to do with the expedition.[1]

It is summer in the southern hemisphere. Shouldn't the ice have melted? It is entertaining that a ship out to talk about global warming should get stuck in ice. Poetic justice. It reminds me of the Global Warming hearing that was canceled last March because of a snowstorm. If this sort of thing persists for a few more years, the climate change lobby will start saying we are headed for a man-made ice age and only new government regulations and taxes can save us.

Then there is this:

Cold facts: More record lows than highs in USA in 2013

"For the first year since 1993, there were more daily record lows than daily highs that were either tied or set in 2013," reported Weather Channel meteorologist Guy Walton, who keeps track of the data from the climate center.

Through Dec. 28, there have been 11,852 daily record lows in 2013, compared with 10,073 daily record highs, according to Walton.[2]

Records only go back to the 1880s and this is only the first time in 20 years that lows outnumbered highs but it is an interesting point on the graph. The climate is on a cycle measured in centuries or even millennia, not decades.

Sunday, January 19, 2014

Dredd vs. Judge Dredd

Dredd

Judge Dredd made his return to film and I finally got around to seeing it. A massive improvement over the Stallone version (1995). Whereas Judge Dredd sought to tell an epic tale that glimpsed wide swaths of the Judge Dredd universe, it failed to stay true to the characters or the setting. Dredd tackles a day in the life of a Megacity Judge

The particular day follows Dredd as he takes a rookie recruit on her assessment. Depending how she does, she will either washout or become a judge. As it happens, they find themselves stuck in a mega skyscraper (200 stories and 75,000 residents) with every armed thug out for their blood. The standard judge sidearm, the Lawgiver, gets great play through the movie. Dredd himself proves to be a humorless hard ass who talks like Dirty Harry (FYI: Judge Dredd was modeled on Dirty Harry in a futuristic setting). Of most note, Dredd never removes his helmet.

The recruit, Judge Anderson, is a significant character in the comic and is part of the Psi-Division. Here, she is painted as a mutant with beneficial mutations; there is no Psi-Division. This is really her story since she is the one with the character arc. Dredd is law and the law doesn't need a character arc.

The newer movie lacks the technology of the comic or the Stallone movie. The comic had advanced robotics, flying cars, interplanetary travel, laser rifles, and more. Dredd feels almost modern; much of the missing high-tech is probably for budgetary reasons. One thing that struck me as odd was the ending. Dredd comes upon Mama and she has the building wired to explode if her heart stops. Dredd has already pronounced a death sentence on her. So, stand off? Well, Dredd comes up with a solution that struck me as needlessly risky. I would have just arrested her, had the explosives disarmed while she was carted off to jail. The death sentence can wait a couple of days, can't it? Mama seems to be of the impression that Dredd must execute her on the spot or walk away and leave her alone. Dredd seems to be of the same impression.

Judge Dredd

The Sylvester Stallone epic was much more ambitious than Dredd, including a vast number of characters and plotlines from the long running comic. His disgraced and imprisoned clone, Rico, plays the main villain though his return is entirely unlike what was in the comic. The robot wars are referenced and a warrior robot shows up as a goon for Rico. Fergee is included as a sidekick though he is entirely unlike the character in the comic. The Angel Gang of the Cursed Earth is tossed into the mix as well.

The technology is more in keeping with the comic, though it does seem interplanetary travel has been nixed; Rico was imprisoned on the moon of Titan, not a penal facility in Aspen, Colorado. The costume was more in line with the comic, with the ludicrous shiny shoulder pads. Dredd had toned down the armor which was probably the better move; what works in a comic is often silly in a movie – I give you *The Phantom* (1996) in his purple jumpsuit.

The movie has many failings. First, there is the needless inclusion of a comic sidekick, especially since it was played by Rob Schneider. He is rarely funny. Once they get back to Megacity, I have no idea why he sticks with Dredd. Certainly not because they did some great bonding in the Cursed Earth. There is also the fact that Stallone is very unlike the character he is playing. The constant "I knew you'd say that" is meant to be funny but is just silly. He can't wait to get his helmet off and it stays off through much of the movie. Dredd is the most successful judge in his time and this is repeatedly demonstrated in the comic but Stallone's Dredd is great because he is said to be great. Another issue is that Rico and Dredd are clones but played by different actors; shouldn't they both be played by the same actor?

The movie is generally fun but drifts far from the source material. Dredd is a more modest film but does a much better job of staying true to the character and the setting.

The Overrated Martin Scorsese

Yet again, Martin Scorsese has released a ridiculously long film (3 hours) about a miserable human being and it is an Oscar contender, highly rated by the critics, and cleaning up at the box office. I am generally baffled. I have seen many of his films and don't understand the appeal. I have concluded that Scorsese's signature as director is similar to Picasso's signature on a painting; even complete crap is instantly valuable.

Taxi Driver (1976)

I saw this a few years ago and was less than impressed. Our hero is a deranged taxi driver who is baffled that a pretty girl doesn't want to go to a porno movie with him and thinks he can turn his life around by killing an aspiring politician. That plan falls through but he still wants to shoot somebody so he kills a pimp and his goons. Voila! He really is a hero who saved a young girl from prostitution. There were no characters to like in this film. But see, after he killed a bunch of people, he is a changed man. Look how calm and collected he is now.

Raging Bull (1980)

This was the first Scorsese film I saw. It was in the theaters as a double feature with The Elephant Man (sheesh, two black and white films!). I was 13 and didn't like either film. Jake LaMotta was a real jerk and I couldn't figure why his wife endured him. This from a 13 year old kid!

The King of Comedy (1982)

Here is yet another movie with De Niro as the star, this time with the unlikely name of Rupert Pupkin. Rupert thinks he's a comic genius and has it in his head that he should get a shot on famous late night show (hosted by Jerry Lewis). To pull it off, he kidnaps Jerry. Yes, another mentally deranged character. Though supposedly a comedy, I didn't laugh. I've never liked Jerry Lewis and yet he is the brightest point in this travesty.

The Color of Money (1986)

I saw this when it was in theaters and have almost no recollection of it. About the only thing that I recall was Forest Whitaker hustling Paul Newman toward the end. Of course, it is a movie about pool sharks, not exactly folks of high moral character; in other words, right up Scorsese's alley. He has a habit of glamorizing morally bankrupt people (more on that later).

The Last Temptation of Christ (1988)

How did I see this movie? I must have rented it from Blockbuster back in the day when I'd rent 4 movies a week. Well, here is a telling of Christ in which Judas Iscariot proves to be a hero and Jesus skips out on the crucifixion in order to marry Mary and grow old. I like Willem Dafoe but, at this time, he was almost always a villain so casting him as Jesus was impolitic. And, despite being about Jesus, there are no likable characters. How can that be?

Goodfellas (1990)

I somehow suffered through this two and a half hour glorification of really bad people. You know, I felt nothing when Pesci got whacked. He was a bad guy. Sure, he could be funny but he's still murdering scum. Ditto for our other main characters. Am I supposed to identify with one of these thugs? Scorsese sure wants to impress me with their lifestyle. That tracking shot of getting a front table at the posh club was nothing if not impressive. See the special consideration these mobsters got? Isn't that cool? Stuck in witness protection, Henry Hill misses the excitement of his old life. What, am I supposed to feel sorry for him?

Cape Fear (1991)

Here is one I saw in the theaters as an adult, making it the first of his films that I chose to see. I thought the filming was interesting, especially when Nolte was shaving in the foreground and Lange was in the background yet both were in focus. That was cool and the first I had seen of that sort of thing. However, as usual, I didn't like any of the characters. This was Juliette Lewis's big break and I was not at all impressed. How is it she had a long career?

The Age of Innocence (1993)

Oh, the tedium! Every setting has to be lovingly explained by narration, pointing out the table settings and the tablecloth and the who's who stuff. It is like lives of the rich and famous in the late 19th century. Worse, our characters are all so staid and proper that seldom does emotion actually leak through the façade. The characters are so stolid and the setting so sterile that it is near impossible to feel anything for any of these characters.

Bringing out the Dead (1999)

Dreary and bleak, this movie was hard to watch. Nick Cage plays a depressed emergency medical tech who goes from one disaster to the next, hallucinating on the way. Gee, why am I watching this? Grim and unrewarding. Oh, but he does manage to fall asleep at the end.

Gangs of New York (2002)

OMG, it's still going! When the movie started, I was interested. And when it came to the big finale where DiCaprio is going to knife Day-Lewis, I was still there. And then he failed. And Day-Lewis let him live. And the movie just kept going. And going. Come on, already! At 167 minutes, the movie is just too long. And yet again, all the characters are thugs and villains. Should I root for the bad guy or the bad guy? Roger Ebert once said a good movie can never be too long and a bad one can never be short enough. Most directors try handing in a final film that is near three hours and the studio will demand huge cuts. Not Scorsese. And it doesn't benefit the narrative for the films to be so damned long.

The Aviator (2004)

This film was so enthralling that I never finished it. I watched about half of it then lost interest. Cate Blanchet made a good Kathryn Hepburn. As far as Hughes, I tired of him and changed channels. Here is one of the great achievers of the 20th Century, a man who broke airspeed records, who designed aircraft, who made blockbuster films, who was a successful businessman, a philanthropist, and yet the biopic bored me. Also, as usual, I didn't like anyone. Why is it I don't like any characters in a Scorsese film? How does he pull that off, film after film?

Shutter Island (2010)

Though I didn't have a heads up or read any spoilers, I knew the twist to this film in the first five minutes. In fact, I knew he was the man he was looking for when he looked in the mirror with his freshly washed face. I was sitting in the theater trying to figure out if Teddy Daniels could be rearranged to spell Andrew

Laeddis. Of course, it didn't work because his name is Edward Daniels; used Teddy to throw me. Again, the film is way too long, the setting is filled with paranoia (it is a mental hospital), and everyone is under suspicion. When the big secret is revealed, I rolled my eyes. Oh, look, another nutbag for our main character. Gee, you've never tried that before. Sigh.

Hugo (2011)

This was generally interesting and entertaining though overly slow and, in the end, infuriating. We follow young Hugo, an orphan who finds himself winding clocks in a Parisian train station and trying to avoid the comically bumbling policeman and his dog. During this, he attempts to unwrap a riddle with a little mechanical toy his father left him. Slowly we discover that a humble shopkeeper in the train station is Georges Melies, an early pioneer in film. Suddenly, the film becomes a paean to Georges Melies! Huh? I first learned of Georges Melies in *From the Earth to the Moon* (HBO Series) and was truly impressed by his achievement. Clearly, Scorsese shares my feelings. However, why not just make a film about Georges Melies rather than this meandering mess that concludes with a thumbnail sketch of the great filmmaker? I suppose this is one of his least bad movies since I liked Hugo well enough.

The average length of a Scorsese film is 133 minutes, he often tells stories about the mentally deranged or criminals and doesn't do an effective job of creating empathy for them. Clearly, I am in a minority on this. What amazes me about Scorsese is that I don't like any of his films. I generally dislike Jim Jarmusch films (Limits of Control was tedious and Dead Man was unwatchable) but I really like Ghost Dog: Way of the Samurai. The same goes for several other directors but not Scorsese. Somehow, I dislike all his movies, at least the ones I've seen.

What do you think? Am I totally wrong? If so, please explain.

Monday, January 20, 2014

Wolf of Wall Street

An actual victim of Jordan Belfort complains that the movie glorifies the wolf's crimes.

The real life 'Wolf of Wall Street': behind the Scorsese film

Few watching The Wolf of Wall Street will have known that the real-life fraudster on whom it is based sold the film rights to his memoir of the same name – nor that hundreds of his real-life victims are still

awaiting compensation. Jacqui Goddard hears from some of them[3]

This is such a common theme for Scorsese and a big reason why I don't like his films.

Tuesday, January 21, 2014

Star Trek Into Darkness

Our story opens on an alien planet where a figure in a gray robe flees from a temple while the natives chase him, throwing spears on the way. The figure proves to be Captain James T Kirk who had stolen – for reasons never explained – a scroll from said temple thus the ire of the natives. Gee, this almost looks like the opening scene from Raiders of the Lost Ark. Kirk soon joins Dr. McCoy and the pair continues to run for their lives. What was the plan here? Meanwhile, Spock, Sulu, and Uhura are in a shuttle hovering over an active volcano located next to the temple. Spock is lowered into the volcano so he can plant a device to prevent it from erupting and thus wiping out the natives. Well, things don't work quite as planned. The shuttle engines overheat and the tether to Spock breaks. Was there a plan here? Simple, we just beam Spock to the ship. Where's the Enterprise? Oh, it is underwater! Kirk and Bones jump off a cliff and swim down to the submerged *SPACE* ship. Though Scotty was able to beam Sulu and Uhura to safely before the shuttle crashed, he can't lock onto Spock except by line of sight. The ship's current position is a real problem, seeing as there is ocean and continent in the way. What genius decided to park the ship in an ocean? Well, since we are in this really stupid position, the only way to save Spock is to break the Prime Directive (note that was the Prime directive, not the secondary or tertiary directive). The ship surfaces to the natives' astonishment and as it flies over the volcano, Spock is beamed aboard. And there you have the introduction to J. J. Abrams' latest travesty in the Star Trek universe.

Knowing that the objective was to prevent the volcano from erupting and wiping out the primitive natives, what might have been a better plan? Maybe setting the anti-volcano device on a several second delay and transporting it from orbit? Oh, but look at all the awesome action we'd miss! As for Kirk stealing the holy scroll, I am still baffled. Why? My best guess is that he was trying to lure the natives away from the impending detonation. Even so, I have no idea why Bones would be there. Is he particularly suited to running from natives? The sad thing is that it gets worse.

Lacking any original ideas, the writers bring back Khan (i.e. *Star Trek II: The Wrath of Khan*) as a villain. Khan has magic blood that appears to be a cure for death. Yep, Dr. McCoy synthesizes a serum that revives a dead tribble and maybe a major character that dies in a scene stolen from… Wrath of Khan. I was really annoyed when the last film had Kirk and Scotty beam aboard the Enterprise while it was light years away and traveling at warp speed. This time, we have a personal transportation device that allows the villain to transport himself from Earth to the Klingon home world! Really? Such technology is going to make starships obsolete. Such a technology would massively revolutionize space travel and is far beyond what was possible in *Star Trek The Next Generation*. As for the starships, warp speed has really gotten impressive. The ship is a short distance from the Klingon home world – which the Klingons seem not to notice – and warps back toward Earth. They have hardly hit warp speed when an enemy ship catches them and blasts the Enterprise. So, where are we? Oh, pretty much in Earth orbit. So the distance from Earth to the Klingon home world is a few minutes at warp speed? Two starships are essentially in Earth orbit and one fires at the other. Earth responds by doing nothing. One of the starships is on a collision course with San Francisco and the response is… nothing. We have all of Earth and the only people who can do anything are the crew of the Enterprise.

Benedict Cumberbatch seems nothing like Khan. First, it is a bit annoying that we have a pasty white fellow playing Khan. But Khan had a combination of charm and menace, a man who would smile warmly while he twisted the knife. Cumberbatch is all menace and brooding.

Scotty goes scouting coordinates that Kirk gave him. He finds a space station there. Amazingly, the space station doesn't seem to notice him. In a miracle of timing, some ships arrive and enter the space station – Scotty just joins the group and enters unseen.

Seriously? This is a military space station and it neither noticed the approach of a shuttle or that the shuttle came aboard. Well, such incompetence probably explains later parts of the film.

So, Scotty is off the ship and Kirk needs a new chief engineer. Let's see, I have all these engineers down in engineering, one of whom is probably second only to Scotty. So, let's pick Chekov. Yes, I understand you don't want to introduce new characters but this still grated.

Spock and Uhura are involved and their relationship is repeatedly brought to the foreground, often with Uhura nagging Spock for his logic and lack of feelings. Umm, you know he's a Vulcan, right? But, just to prove he's got feelings, a tear runs down his cheek when a major character dies. Oh, and Kirk cries too when a different character dies. I don't think William Shatner's Kirk ever cried, even when those Klingon bastards killed his son. The Spock – Uhura relationship was ill-conceived.

Chris Pine's Kirk is disappointing. It's not that I think he should emulate Shatner, but it would be nice if he kept to the character. His Kirk is frantic rather than deliberate, foolhardy rather than brave, and reckless rather than daring. At one point, we see him in bed with two alien women. Really? He has to be convinced not to do something rash on more than one occasion. At another point in the movie, he is faced with the Kobayashi Maru moment where he's going to lose his ship and crew and his response is… "I'm sorry." In Wrath of Khan, Kirk repeatedly outmaneuvered Khan but here it is the other way around. Kirk captures him only because he chose to surrender. Kirk survives a spacewalk only because Khan guides him, and Kirk survives secondary villains only because of Khan. Khan plays Kirk the entire time but Kirk blusters as if he is the one in control. Sigh.

The plot is just an opportunity to string together unlikely action sequences. There is an amazing amount of running! It's all very exciting mindless fun. And that is the biggest problem. Star Trek was never mindless. If anything, the Kirk era of Star Trek was preachy with a morality tale in virtually every episode. Kirk often explained the moral at the end. If there is any moral here, it is that the enemy is us. Yeah. Again with the self-loathing and we made Khan what he is and those chickens have come home to roost. Lovely.

With what J. J. Abrams has done to Star Trek, I am concerned what he plans to do with the other great sci-fi classic, Star Wars. Well, he probably can't do any worse than Lucas did in *Phantom Menace*.

There's no voter fraud

Last week Al Sharpton embraced convicted vote fraudster Melowese Richardson at a "voting rights" rally in Cincinnati. The United States Department of Justice under Eric Holder has done nothing to Melowese Richardson 410 days after she admitted on camera that she committed multiple federal felonies by voting six times for President Obama's reelection.

Federal law makes it a felony to vote more than once for President. In fact, 42 U.S.C. Section 1973i(e) subjects Richardson to twenty-five years in federal prison for her six votes for Obama.[4]

Clearly, there is no need for voter ID. Also, it seems if you vote for the right person, voter fraud isn't a crime.

Racism according to Kareem

It turns out that since his basketball career, Kareem Abdul-Jabbar has become a contributor to Time Magazine. Who knew? He comments on how to tell if you are a racist. If you've ever said that you don't care if someone is white, black, yellow, or purple, he suggests that's a hint you may be racist. He says that the issue may be how we define racism. Then, in the rest of the article, he fails to define racism. Awesome. However, he does list things that he thinks are racist. Topping his list is that you deny there is racism. Well, there's a straw man. No one denies there is racism. Racism was codified into the legal system prior to the Civil Rights Movement. That was structural, wide-spread racism that needed to be stamped out. Today, we have buffoons like Donald Sterling. The magnitude of that change is profound but Kareem isn't having it. See, the Supreme Court overturned part of the Voting Rights Act. Racism! The Supreme Court has weakened Affirmative Action. Racism! Bill O'Reilly says that discrimination is in the past. Racism! He offers a 2006 poll (couldn't come up with something more recent?) that showed 49% of minorities think racism is a big problem versus only 18% of whites. Racism!

Racism today is a pale shadow to what it once was. How else to explain that a black man is president, that a black woman was Secretary of State under a Republican president, that Oprah Winfrey spent decades as the most popular television personality? Why is it that immigrant blacks do amazingly well within a generation while native ones struggle? I would posit that the immigrants haven't spent a lifetime being marinated in talk of racism from people like Al Sharpton, Jessie Jackson, Spike Lee, and Kareem Abdul-Jabbar. Stop telling blacks that they are victims of racism and slavery and The Man. Instead, tell them that they can be President, Attorney General, Secretary of State, UN Ambassador, Supreme Court Justice, or whatever else. Will there be hurdles? Of course! It certainly doesn't help that anyone who opposes the president's policies is automatically a racist. If that is how you define racism, then you will find a lot of racists. Worse still, any black person who opposes the president is an Uncle Tom or a Race Traitor.

To a hammer, everything is a nail. To someone like Kareem Abdul-Jabbar, everything is racism.

Friday, May 23, 2014

Godzilla

I remember watching Godzilla movies fairly regularly as a kid. In the early versions, Godzilla was a giant monster bent on the destruction of Tokyo and could not be stopped by any of the high-tech tanks and planes sent against him. Later, Godzilla morphed into a hero, saving Japan from other wicked giant monsters. I suspect there was some continuity to that which I have long since forgotten or perhaps never knew. The new Godzilla is in the later mold.

The movie is mostly about the unluckiest family alive: the Brody's. I suspect these Brody's are somehow related to Sheriff Brody of the Jaws movies. Joe Brody and his wife work at a nuclear plant in Japan. Though they don't know it at the time, it suffers a meltdown because of a giant monster nesting beneath it. 15 years later, Joe's son, Lt. Ford Brody, has just come home from a tour of duty - he is with Explosive Ordinance Disposal (EOD) - when he gets a call that his father has been arrested in Japan. He goes to Japan and ends up at the site of the meltdown just as a giant monster awakens and wreaks havoc. Heading home, Ford stops in Hawaii, where he finds himself on the battlefield of giant monsters! But he escapes that and gets back to California just in time to run into a giant monster! His son is on a bus on the Golden Gate Bridge when a giant monster swims into the bay! His wife is hiding in a subway station when giant monsters start fighting in the streets of San Francisco!

I did like that the monsters feed on radiation. They like nothing more than some tasty nuclear waste. Also, they have this natural defense of an EMP (electromagnetic pulse) which dramatically limits the ability of the military to attack them. There is a scene where aircraft just fall out of the sky and all the lights go out. I still think a naval gun should be able to take them down but at least there is some reason why the military is confounded by them. Godzilla is immense. He is the biggest version to date. I liked what they did with the jagged plates on his back but his face looks too much like a dog. It was cool that his emerging from the ocean caused a tsunami.

The monster fights really take off in the final act and something about the action reminded me of those Godzilla movies of yore. Though it was done with topflight computer graphics, the way the monsters crash into buildings just seemed like some guy was in a monster suit. This was likely an homage to those original films.

I went into the movie with low expectations (I saw the last *Godzilla* movie with Matthew Broderick) and was quite surprised to find it was a good movie. I expect that Godzilla will return to battle more giant monsters that plague the earth. I can hardly wait.

Saturday, May 31, 2014

Valerie Plame Redux

Remember when Robert Novak mentioned Valerie Plame, wife of Joe Wilson, in an article. This mention soon became a national scandal that put Scooter Libby in jail and painted the

Bush Administration as bullying Wilson's wife to get revenge for his contrary report on Nigerian yellow cake. As the story goes, Plame was a CIA agent and releasing her name made her a target. Also, it's illegal to reveal the identity of an undercover agent. Of course, she wasn't undercover and the law didn't apply. Also, it was eventually revealed that Richard Armitage - not Scotter Libby - leaked her name to Novak. But, as mentioned, that wasn't illegal and thus he was never prosecuted. This faux scandal spawned a movie (*Fair Game*, 2010). What we can glean from this is that the press takes it extremely seriously if a CIA agent is revealed, even if that agent is not covert.

Last week, the Obama Administration revealed the name of the Afghan CIA station chief, a person who is (was) covert. Unlike Plame, this is a real leak. Where is Patrick Fitzgerald? Clearly, someone in the Obama White House needs to be jailed and the rest of the administration needs to be harassed. What, the story is over already? Didn't the Plame story go on from months and years? Did someone at least get fired? No?

It is good to see the press showing balance in how they treat a Republican administration vs. a Democrat administration.

Wednesday, June 4, 2014

Iran-Contra Redux

For those of you old enough, do you recall the firestorm that ensued when it was discovered that the US was giving weapons to Iran, who then 'intervened' on our behalf to get hostages released? Hostage-taking was a popular pastime for Middle Eastern terrorists in the 1980s. This was THE big scandal of the Reagan Administration and it lingered for his second term and into the Bush presidency. Reagan had proclaimed that the US did not negotiate with terrorists and yet Iran-Contra contradicted that.

The Obama Administration has gone one better. Rather than trading arms to Qatar to get them to convince the Taliban to release Sgt. Bowe Bergdahl (which would have been about equivalent to that aspect of Iran-Contra), the administration has released 5 terrorists from Gitmo who will spend a 1 year parole in Qatar before being released to resume their terror careers. Much as Iran-Contra was a breach of the Boland Amendment, the Bergdahl-Taliban swap broke the law when Congress wasn't kept in the loop. Now, if we were trading a handful of mid-level Nazis to get back a General Patton, I might be inclined to support the president. Instead, we have traded an interior minister/Taliban co-founder, a chief of staff, a provincial governor, a deputy intelligence chief, and a member of a joint Al Qaeda-Taliban cell for a deserter who should be court martialed. Well played, Taliban. Well played.

Worse still, President Obama hyped this with a Rose Garden appearance. He's running a victory lap over this. Is he daft? The president does stuff like this on a regular basis. He distracts the media from bad news by provided some new bad news. There are so many scandals that it is impossible to cover them. Like a school of fish, it is hard to focus on just one. The media, which has a short attention span, is never given the opportunity to delve too deeply into a scandal. What were we talking about before Bergdahl? Oh yeah, the VA scandal. What ever happened to the IRS targeting scandal? Fast and Furious? Collecting phone records of the Associated Press? Naming a reporter a co-conspirator to tap his phone? "If you like your doctor, you can keep your doctor" scandal? Benghazi? How about the collapsing foreign policy where the US is being played by Vladimir Putin? It goes on and on. There is so much that the populace has thrown up its hands.

Friday, June 13, 2014

Obama Achievement: Iraq Collapse

Three years ago when the President pulled the entirety of US forces out of Iraq, Vice President Biden declared this a great accomplishment of the administration. We skedaddled and left the Iraqis to fend for themselves; mission accomplished. Well, as Reverend Wright might say, those chickens have come home to roost. Mosul has fallen to a branch of Al Qaeda.

Whether one agreed with the mission or not, thousands of Americans died to secure a democracy in the heart of the Muslim world. I myself did not like the plan. Short of a McArthur-esque dictatorship, I view nation building as a doomed project. Nonetheless, we spent years doing it and had more success than I expected. Then we left. By leaving, we abandoned whatever 'investments' were made and we see the result. After WWII, we stayed in Germany. 70 years later, we are still in Germany and it is a functioning Western democracy. After Korea, we stayed in South Korea. We are still there. It is a hugely successful country compared to its neighbor, North Korea. Look at the difference between the part of Korea where the US stayed and the part that we lost. After Vietnam, we left South Vietnam. Catastrophe followed. The record is pretty clear.

The US has lost prestige under Obama and no one can trust us. Obama has betrayed allies and appeased enemies. He has abandoned the idea of US leadership in the world. Putin has made a fool of Obama and Obama appears not to mind. Here is a president who was dealt a Straight Flush, discarded it, and asked for 5 new cards. It is hard to credit this as mere incompetence. Is the destruction of US foreign policy intentional, thus crippling future efforts? Who can trust the US now? We might just elect another Obama and abandon whoever counts on us.

Thursday, June 19, 2014

You don't have mail

There are times when I am astonished at the stories the administration will tell. As an IT guy who has a basic understanding of email, I look at the story of Lois Lerner's lost emails on account of a hard drive crash as an obvious lie. We use Exchange at my work. My email is not on my computer, it is on the Exchange server. It is also in the inbox to whomever it was sent. So, unless Ms. Lerner only sent email to herself, one hard drive failure can't destroy any of her emails. Our server has multiple backups in case of failure and the data is backed up to tapes should the building burn down. I was doing this sort of backup 16 years ago, which makes it unbelievable that the IRS isn't doing it today. How many hard drives, servers, and offsite tape backups would have to be destroyed or fail to get rid of Ms. Lerner's emails? A lot more than the one that is claimed. This story is even worse since most people must see that it doesn't make sense. Your average smartphone user can access email on the phone, or on the computer, or even on a tablet. Most know that if their computer crashes, they haven't just lost all their emails.

If these emails really have been lost, it is because someone chose to lose them. That would be a crime. Why commit a crime to hold back these emails? Much like Nixon's tapes, there is something in those emails the administration or the IRS doesn't want revealed. If this same thing happened in a Republican administration, the media would be howling day and night. This cover-up is so obvious as to insult the intelligence of anyone with even a moderate amount of tech savvy.

Saturday, June 21, 2014

Email Archiving! What a concept!

Came across this link on Instapundit:

The IRS Had a Contract With an Email Backup Company

The IRS had a contract with email backup service vendor Sonasoft starting in 2005[5]

The IRS has had an email backup solution since 2005 with a company that advertises as 'Email Archiving Done Right.' Huh. Either this company is going to take a major hit for such a huge - and growing - failure or it might say, "Here they are."

Again, the idea that the emails are lost is ludicrous and will only convince the ignorant or willfully blind. This is an obvious cover-up. I'm sure the media would be equally understanding if a Republican administration apparently used the IRS to squash opposition and then stonewalled a Congressional investigation.

Sunday, June 22, 2014

Global Warming Hoax Revealed! Yet Again!

The scandal of fiddled global warming data

The US has actually been cooling since the Thirties, the hottest decade on record

When future generations try to understand how the world got carried away around the end of the 20th century by the panic over global warming, few things will amaze them more than the part played in stoking up the scare by the fiddling of official temperature data. There was already much evidence of this seven years ago, when I was writing my history of the scare, The Real Global Warming

Disaster.[6]

Who has been saying that it is a hoax so the government can coax more tax dollars out of your pocket? And who has been cooking the numbers? A government agency! If your grants and awards depend on a continued warming trend, you will find a way to make sure the numbers show warming. However, eventually the truth will out. Of course, the truth has been out for years but there are so many who are willfully blind to the fact. Once invested in a belief, it is very hard to let it go, regardless of the evidence.

Friday, June 27, 2014

Electoral Shenanigans

Thad Cochran, Senator from Mississippi, recently won a runoff election against Chris McDaniel, a Tea Party challenger. Of interest, he only won thanks to the votes of black democrats who took part in the Republican primary. This is one reason I think open primaries are silly since it allows the other party to potentially choose its competitor. However, those are the rules and it can bite both ways. So far, so good. But now it turns out that the Republicans were behind this. Former Governor Hailey Barbour's nephew was involved in getting black Democrats to vote against McDaniel by selling the idea that the Tea Party candidate would bring back segregation. Really?

Looking at the numbers, the Tea Party candidate got more Republican votes than Thad did. It was Democrat voters who gave Thad the win. That is not good for the party. Thad will not get those Democrats to vote for him in the November election and these shenanigans may have convinced many Republicans to sit out the election. Republicans and Democrats will join forces to defeat Tea Party candidates. Why?

Of course, both parties have already said that the Tea Party is "far right-wing" and "racist." For the uninformed, that is enough. In fact, the Tea Party generally has 3 goals: Constitutional

restoration, responsible budgeting, and economic freedom.[7] Our government has long since breached the limits of the Constitution but has recently become tyrannical. The government needs to shrink back to the specified limits of the

Constitution. Next, the overspending has gotten out of hand and the huge deficits spell doom if not reined in. Lastly, there must be a return to economic freedom. There has been entirely too much regulation and corporatism (aka crony capitalism) in recent years. The government should not be deciding which businesses prosper and which don't. Entrenched politicians of both parties dislike these goals since it inevitably strips them of power. Few willingly surrender power; doing so is what made George Washington so great.

Monday, June 30, 2014

What a Tangled Web Government Weaves

Oh, the horror. The Supreme Court has ruled 5-4 that the government cannot require religious people to provide something against their religious beliefs just because they opened a business. Now, rather than having their employer pay for their contraceptives, some women (those who *voluntarily* chose employment at Hobby Lobby or likeminded corporations) will have to pay for them. Yes, the horror, the tragedy. Next, it will be rent, food, car insurance, and cable TV. What, the employer doesn't pay for any of those? Huh.

I have long held that the corporation should provide nothing but a paycheck. How the employee chooses to spend the money is then no business of the business. You want health insurance, buy health insurance. You want condoms, buy condoms. The moment you force others to purchase your desires, it is inevitable that there will be conflict. Furthermore, if someone else is buying it, the person using it has no incentive to keep costs down. If someone else was paying the phone bill, will the user pay attention to roaming charges? No. This is always the problem with third party payers. And that leads to rationing, like we see at the VA. Unable to meet the demand, the VA would force veterans to wait long periods before getting care.

How did it come about that healthcare was provided by business? Government interference in the market. Yes, the government decided to play around with wage and price controls. Always trying to find ways around such government meddling, businesses started offering 'benefits' that weren't classified as wages. Voila! Therefore, our current mess is the result of previous government efforts to fix things. It worked out so well that the government needs to fix it again. And that has worked out so well that President Obama has issued hundreds of waivers, multiple rewrites of the law, delays of enforcement, and accusations of Republican intransigence.

Government fixes usually lead to unforeseen problems that call for another government fix that leads to unforeseen problems that call for a government fix. This process goes on until the government has complete control of an underperforming and wasteful industry, like education or Amtrak. A better option is to get the government out of these industries (for which there is no Constitutional authority, by the way) and let private companies innovate.

Friday, July 11, 2014

Impeachment Folly

Again there are calls to impeach the president and I can only shake my head. Short of Obama gunning down a citizen on camera (who is not a Republican), the Democratically controlled Senate will not convict. Therefore, impeachment can only end in failure. Might the process moderate President Obama's lawlessness? Doubtful. No, it will most likely just irritate the voters and boost Democrat turnout. It is a terrible idea with no path to success.

Does Obama merit impeachment? Certainly. It may be recalled that I considered bailing out the car companies as impeachable and no one even considers that today. He has rewritten immigration law, enforcing the Dreamer Law that Congress declined to pass. He has rewritten the Affordable Care Act, also without Congressional involvement. He went to war in Libya without Congressional authorization; Bush got authorization for both Afghanistan and Iraq. But, as with criminal courts, the District Attorney should not take a case to trial that it is certain he will lose. It is a waste of time and money.

What of this lawsuit that the Speaker of the House is pushing? It is only necessary because the Republicans have proven again and again to be spineless. The House has the power of the purse. Nothing can be funded unless a majority of the House votes for it. Once the Republicans took the House, Obamacare was dead. Well, it was dead if they had spines. No, they folded again and again. The Republicans voted to fund Obamacare because they couldn't make the case that the Democratic Senate was shutting down the government. Having surrendered the power of the purse, the House Republicans are now going to beg the courts to force the president to enforce the laws that the Congress did pass, not the ones he wished had passed. Weakness.

Wednesday, July 30, 2014

E. T. the Extra-Terrestrial

32 years after I first saw it in theaters, I saw *E. T. the Extra-Terrestrial* again on the big screen. I do not recall my thoughts on the film all those many years ago. Seeing it again, I found it generally entertaining but also a bit silly. In the opening, we see that E. T. has wandered far from his spacecraft and is unable to get back before it blasts back into space. Fine, he's got these stumpy legs and walks only slightly faster than a turtle. However, he did move with astonishing speed under cover of bushes when trying to get back to his ship. How does that work? But that is beside the point. The big issue is that we discover he can fly! We only see him fly when he is in the basket of Eliot's bicycle but one supposes he could fly without the added weight. So, if he can fly, shouldn't he have been able to get back to his ship?

You are an alien on an alien world. You are a highly advanced being who can make an interstellar communicator out of children's toys, coffee cans, and an umbrella. You know you are hunted by some of the native population but have managed to befriend several children. You have the house to yourself while the family is away. Do you a) work on a plan to reunite with your people or b) get falling-down drunk on the local inebriating drink? E. T. chose plan b. Maybe he isn't one of the brighter aliens. In fact, many of his actions do paint him as a dimwit among star-hopping astronauts.

E.T. builds a distress beacon that will summon his people to rescue him from this harsh world. Both he and Eliot are ill as they sit in the woods. Eliot falls asleep. Does E.T. a) remain close to Eliot and the beacon or b) wander off and fall into a creek for the night to exacerbate his illness? Plan b it is.

E. T. manages to fake his death. Perhaps it wasn't fake and his species just resurrects after death. In any case, he has fooled the dullards that he is dead. Left alone with only the young boy who is his ally, does he a) quietly slip away with Eliot's aide or b) make a ruckus that will attract the humans but for Eliot's intervention? Yeah, plan b again.

It does seem that E.T. is an idiot-savant, at once brilliant and then a complete buffoon. I can just imagine the aliens on the ship muttering about how that half-wit Zreck wandered off again. They probably decided to leave him behind to teach him a lesson. "Let's go explore the moons of Jupiter and come back to get Zreck in a few days." Snicker snicker.

Luckily, it turns out that the humans are also idiots. You know there is an alien hiding in the neighborhood and use all sort of high-tech gizmos to ferret him out. You discover his emergency beacon still sending a signal. Do you a) leave a bunch of guys there in case the ship shows up or b) get totally surprised when it shows up? Oh, look, it landed in EXACTLY the same spot where it did last time. Hmmm.

'Keys' (Peter Coyote) has wanted to meet an alien since he was 10. He is eager to make peaceful contact, or so he tells Eliot. With that in mind, should he a) move slowly and embody a non-threatening manner or b) arrive in a cavalry of off-road vehicles flashing high-beams and run after any movement with flashlights sweeping the forest like klieg lights? He chose plan b .

It was funny to see C. Thomas Howell as one of the biker boys and Erika Eleniak - future Baywatch vixen - as Eliot's love interest. Of course, Drew Barrymore is adorable as Eliot's younger sister.

When first I saw this, I was not the harsh critic I have become. I liked virtually any movie I saw and never sought out plot holes. Yes, those were innocent days. Now all the plot holes, silliness, and inconsistencies are obvious and often annoying. Still, it was fun to watch it again all these years later. Strange to think this was the highest-grossing movie of the 1980s, a decade that saw *Raiders of the Lost Ark*, *The Empire Strikes Back*, and *Return of the Jedi*.

Monday, August 11, 2014

Romney Returns

I will be the first to say that I would far prefer to have had Mitt Romney as president for the last two years than Barack Obama. That said, he had his shot. He had the best shot of any challenger of a sitting president in more than 30 years. With a disastrous economy, collapsing foreign policy, and high and persistent unemployment, Romney lost. Millions of Republicans sat at home rather than go to the polls and vote Romney. Many of them may be regretting that decision in light of the further collapse of foreign policy (e.g. Ukraine, Iraq, Israel-Palestine) and the still floundering economy but that is not a reason to vote for Romney in 2016.

While ads savaged Romney for the death by cancer of the wife of a man who had several years earlier lost his job and health insurance when Bain Capital closed his factory, Mitt ran no such attack ads against President Obama. There were no ads that the president left Americans to die in Benghazi. There were no ads about Fast and Furious. There weren't even ads about the president's numerous golf outings (playing golf was practically a war crime during the Bush Presidency). McCain ran the same campaign four years earlier and Romney didn't learn from that. Will he play hardball in 2016? I doubt it.

If he can't get votes against someone with an unimpressive four year record, how is he going to get votes against a blank slate? There is a reason that neither party reruns a loser.

Wednesday, September 17, 2014

Scotland Forever

Tomorrow, Scotland will have a vote on whether to break from the United Kingdom. It is a peculiar development since Scotland didn't eagerly join the UK; I don't think Wales or Ireland joined eagerly either. The Act of Union (1707) was mutually agreed upon by both nations. Unlike Wales and Ireland, Scottish kings had ruled in England - the Stuarts - making Union less a conquest than a marriage. However the Scots were led to union on account of a financial disaster. It was a time of colonies in the New World and Scotland wanted to share in the bounty. The country had put itself in great debt for the Darien Scheme which failed miserably. Between disease and hostile Spaniards, the Panamanian colony of Scots was decimated. The English piled on the disaster by seizing a would-be trade vessel. In the wake of the catastrophe, union with England looked better than financial ruin.

Of course, most people probably think about Braveheart and William Wallace. It has been 20 years since Mel Gibson portrayed a clean-shaven Wallace who supposedly had an affair with Princess Isabella and fathered Edward III. Enjoyable though that film was, it was mostly fictional nonsense. However, it did spawn a renewed desire for Scottish independence.

Based on how the Scots vote for parliament, I suspect they will not be pleased with the end result. Oh, sticking it to the English might please them and being the masters of their own destiny will be exciting for a while but Scotland is a small economy that has enjoyed benefits from a larger economy. An independent Scotland will need to raise taxes to maintain the level of government it now enjoys. Moreover, it might find itself shunned by the European Union lest the EU encourage more separatist movements. I think independence would benefit them in the long run but be harsh in the short run.

Of special note, Sean Connery will come home if the Yes party wins.

Sunday, September 21, 2014

Security Breach

A man jumped the fence and made it *into* the White House. How could that possibly happen? That is a failure of such a magnitude that I have a hard time believing it. I would sooner have thought someone had gotten into Fort Knox and run off with a few gold ingots. With this kind of failure, there had best be a handful of firings at the Secret Service.

This is a timely breech of security. Access to the White House is controlled to make sure that no one who intends harm to the President is allowed to enter. By the same reasoning, we have borders and immigration laws. It has been reported that Middle Easterners have been captured crossing the southern border. Most likely, those who have been caught - and the inevitable fraction who slipped through - are only seeking a better life. But we don't know for sure.

Utah Samurai?

Just read the most unexpected headline:

Polygamist women dressed 'like ninjas' attack home of witness in Utah sex assault case[8]

That caught my attention! So I read on...

Two armed "polygamist women" dressed like "ninjas" were subdued by a sword-wielding man during a home invasion, according to police in suburban Utah.

Ninjas against a guy with a sword! Wow, if only this had happened a couple of years ago, it could have been a great episode of Big Love.

Sunday, September 28, 2014

Boyhood

The movie opens with a 7 year-old Mason Evans Jr. (played by Ellar Coltrane) lying in the grass and staring at the clouds. It ends with that same actor 12 years later stating an inanity that he considers profound. That is the shtick of this movie. Over a 12 year period, the same core of actors filmed for 46 days, so about 4 days a year. To watch the kids grow up before you it pretty cool but that doesn't make a film; that makes home movies. If this exact same film were made all at once with multiple actors playing Mason at the various ages of development, it would be widely panned as a boring, going nowhere coming-of-age stinker. The shtick is all this movie has.

Mason starts off as a cute kid but develops into a lost teenager who looks surprisingly unkempt but somehow attracts hot girls. So many scenes go nowhere. At one point, we see Mason being bullied in the boys' restroom and that's an end of that. There is no resolution, no response on his part, just a move to the next part of his life. By the end, Mason is a youth who seems to shrug his shoulders to show emotion and many of his lines include "I guess" or "I don't know."

One message of the film is that fathers suck. Yeah, dads are mostly bad guys, usually drunkards who may even brutalize their wives. Mason's real father (played by Ethan Hawke) is initially an irresponsible doper who eventually gets his act together. But he isn't so much a father as a buddy. There is nothing disciplinary about Mason Sr., just a cool guy and big brother figure.

The message on mothers isn't all that great either. Mason's mom (Patricia Arquette) starts off as a struggling single-mother but she goes back to school to get a degree for a better job. Along the way, she marries one of her professors (the drunken brute) then, after getting her master's degree, she marries one of her students (who is merely a drunk). When Mason leaves for college, she breaks down that her life is over.

Why couldn't he let the characters be apolitical? No, Mason's parents are both Democrats, his father more vociferously so. His father, who only spends a couple weekends a month with them, decided to spend one of those days posting Obama/Biden signs. He even has Mason steal a McCain sign from a yard. Then we have the old man who threatens to shoot Mason for daring to ask if he can post an Obama sign. See, Republicans are nasty, villainous people. Later, we meet an Iraq war vet who says it was a war for oil; he later descends into drunkenness and is written out of the story. See! Look what Bush's War did to the veterans. However, there was a bit of fun poked at Obama supporters; one young mother explains how she sees herself in a make-out session with handsome Senator Obama.

The cultural references were fun, from Mason's sister singing Brittany Spears, to Harry Potter excitement, to Lady Gaga, to the iPhone. Shot as it was provided the ability to give a very accurate view of the given year (no anachronisms to be found).

The shtick is all that carries this movie and it didn't carry it very far for me.

Saturday, October 11, 2014

Foreign Policy Blunder

Iraq asks for US ground troops as Isil threaten Baghdad

Islamic State jihadists move within eight miles of the Iraqi capital, sparking calls for America to return to the country

Iraqi officials have issued a desperate plea for America to bring

US ground troops back to the embattled country, as heavily armed Islamic State militants came within striking distance of Baghdad....[9]

As many predicted, pulling the US military out of Iraq meant it was virtually certain that all the gains achieved would be reversed. Such has come to pass. Unfortunately for Obama, he is still in office. He withdrew the troops, he proudly ran for re-election on the fact that he withdrew the troops, and now Iraq is crumbling.

We stayed in Germany after World War II until... oh, yeah, we're still there. How is Germany doing? We stayed in Japan after WWII until... still there. Japan doing okay? What about South Korea? Still there and it is prospering. Let's look at the places where we didn't stay. Vietnam? It got pretty ugly after we left. How about Haiti? We've sent troops to Haiti many times but they always left. Haiti is a basket case. With this sort of record, why would we choose to leave? It was a virtual guarantee of disaster. But it made for a good campaign slogan for Obama's final election.

There are two strategic options for dealing with ISIS. The first is to fight to win. That would mean ground troops, tanks, re-established bases in Iraq, and a real war. The second is to wash our hands of the matter and let the locals sort it out. Either you want to beat them or you don't. Now, there are also political options. Strategic option 1 is anathema to the Democrat-base in the run-up to a midterm election. Also, option 1 lays bare the blunder in removing troops in the first place. Strategic option 2 is unacceptable because the American people demand some sort of action in the wake of beheaded Americans. Thus we have the political option. We go to war just enough to be 'doing something' but not enough to actually win.

The president's rhetoric has sounded hawkish, claiming we will destroy ISIS. He says that is the goal but he does not provide the means of achieving that end. He is all talk. As the saying goes, actions speak louder than words. Obama's actions, be they with regard to Russia's invasion of the Ukraine, Syria's use of chemical weapons, or a desire to defeat ISIS, always show that his threats are idle. The thugs of the world have a couple years in which to seize power and territory because Obama isn't going to commit to stopping them.

Saturday, November 1, 2014

Terrifying Ignorance

Legal Insurrection went to a college campus and asked students some basic questions:

Who won the Civil War? Only one student answered correctly.

Who is the Vice President? Again, only one student answered correctly after a hint.

Who did we win our independence from? No clue from anyone.

When did we win our independence? No one even close.

The interviewer then shifted to pop culture questions about Snookie, Brad Pitt's current wife, and his former wife. Everyone knew those answers.

How one can be in college and not know this stuff is baffling.

Interesting that they all knew the pop culture questions.[10]

Wednesday, November 5, 2014

Republican Victory? Meh.

Much is being made of the Republican wave in yesterday's elections. The Republicans won the Senate, increased their numbers in the House, and won governorships in 3 blue states. Does this mean things will change? Maybe. Mitch McConnell, the new Majority Leader, said he plans to use the power of the purse. That would be the power that the Republicans won back in 2010 and have repeatedly failed to capitalize upon. Yes, the Democrat Senate torpedoed efforts to defund Obamacare and to hold the line on this spending or that. The Democrat Senate also refused to pass a budget because that would require compromise, so we have spent the last 4 years on continuing resolutions. But now, with a Republican Senate, the Congress will finally pass a budget. Which Obama will almost certainly veto. And the Congress will be unable to override. Which will lead to a looming shutdown. Oh, Mitch McConnell declared he would not allow a shutdown. Therefore, if Obama threatens a shutdown, McConnell has already announced his intent to cave. Yes, this is so much better.

As I have said before, the Republicans are spineless. They will not use the same tactics that Democrats have used against them. Look for rule changes to re-empower the minority in the Senate rather than allow Harry Reid to suffer under the rules he imposed on the Republican minority.

I have railed against Obama for telling ISIS that US ground troops would not be deployed or telling Iran that a military option was off the table with regard to their nuclear program. It hamstrings your ability to reach a diplomatic solution. Criminals surrender to the police because there is a credible threat of force. Imagine if the police declared that they would never draw a gun or a club to subdue a perp. Would that increase or decrease the likelihood of someone resisting arrest?

Obama has crippled his foreign policy by publicly announcing what is and isn't on the table. Mitch McConnell has done the same even before he has taken power. By declaring what you won't do, you assure that that is what your opponent will force you to do. If I were Obama, I would absolutely veto everything to the point of government shutdown and watch the Republicans cave. Duh! And, if I were Putin, I would poke and prod to see just how 'flexible' Obama is after his last election. If I were Iran, I would gladly let Obama browbeat Israel and 'negotiate' with me while my nuclear program advanced unimpeded.

This election was a rejection of the current path of the country and therefore Obama's policies. If it had been a rejection of Republican intransigence, one would have expected a different result. When Bill Clinton suffered a no-confidence vote in 1994, he triangulated and struck a path down the third way. That was more spin than truth but he did compromise. Obama did not compromise after the "shellacking" of 2010 and he won't compromise now.

Two thirds of voters say the country is on the wrong course, which surely guided their vote. With a Republican Congress, we will still continue down that wrong course but there will be a bit more use of the brakes.

Monday, November 10, 2014

Lack of Transparency a Benefit

This bill was written in a tortured way to make sure CBO did not score the mandate as taxes. If [Congressional Budget Office] scored the mandate as taxes, the bill dies. Okay, so it's written to do that. In terms of risk-rated subsidies, if you had a law which said that healthy people are going to pay in -- you made explicit that healthy people pay in and sick people get money — it would not have passed... Lack of transparency is a huge political advantage. And basically, call it the stupidity of the American voter, or whatever, but basically that was really, really critical for the thing to pass. And it's the second-best argument. Look, I wish Mark was right that we could

make it all transparent, but I'd rather have this law than not.[11]

Jonathan Gruber

If the legislation had been clear on what it would do, it would never have passed. Without deception, Obamacare could not have been foisted on the country. And even with the lack of transparency and repeated lies (e.g. "If you like your plan, you can keep your plan"), the law still only passed thanks to legislative legerdemain. The state of Massachusetts, a liberal bastion that hadn't elected a Republican Senator in decades, elected a Republican who ran on the slogan of being the 41st vote to stop Obamacare! And still the Democrats pushed it through and Obama signed it. They knew that the people didn't want it. It was a power grab, an opportunity to take control of a huge portion of the American economy.

Once again, this should be an object lesson. Politicians are rarely interested in serving the people. They are more interested in getting more and more power to tell the people what they must do. The Founders knew that government was more likely to be an oppressor than a benefactor. The bigger it gets, the more tyrannical it can afford to be. What Gruber said here reflects the thoughts of President Obama.

Thursday, October 16, 2014

Ebola

A second nurse from Dallas has come down with Ebola. She has been flown to Atlanta for treatment. The first nurse has been transferred to a facility in Maryland. Both are under strict quarantine to prevent further spread. Of course, they both contracted it from Thomas Duncan who was in quarantine. Not a very effective quarantine, it turns out. Mr. Duncan's family have been quarantined in their apartment for weeks though they have yet to exhibit symptoms. What can we conclude? Quarantine is the best known method for preventing the spread of the virus.

The Ebola outbreak is centered in 3 West African countries. These countries have not been quarantined, which is how Mr. Duncan found his way to a Dallas, Texas. Great Britain has banned travel from the region. Why haven't we? The current panic that is spreading across the country could have been averted if we had a travel ban. Rather than a ban, the government has decided to check the temperature of travelers from the region, a policy that - if in place at the time - would have allowed Thomas Duncan into the country! Are we morons? Moreover, the policy has only been instituted at 5 airports which handle 90 to 95% of all traffic from the region. Therefore, we are allowing 5 to 10% of travelers from Ebola-plagued countries to enter the US without even this inadequate screening?

What of the CDC director? Thomas Frieden was part of former NYC Mayor Bloomberg's bans against large sodas. Here is a man willing to impose policies that will prevent you from drinking too much soda and bringing on health problems years or decades from now but is unwilling to suggest a policy to prevent a virus that has a 50 to 90% fatality rate days after being contracted. If only he could be as determined to prevent Ebola as he is to prevent obesity.

To add to the incomprehensibility of the government response, we are sending thousands of troops to the afflicted regions. To what end? Short of killing off anyone who might be infected (which would be immoral and criminal) like in the opening of the movie Outbreak, the military is just going to put more Americans in the path of the virus. It feels like we are sending the troops in order to claim to be 'doing something' about Ebola. It may not be doing any good but at least action is being taken.

Sunday, November 23, 2014

WMDs in Iraq

Thousands of Iraq Chemical Weapons Destroyed in Open Air, Watchdog Says

The United States recovered thousands of old chemical weapons in Iraq from 2004 to 2009 and destroyed almost all of them in secret and via open-air detonation, according to a written summary of its activities prepared by the Organization for the Prohibition of Chemical Weapons, the international body that monitors

implementation of the global chemical weapons treaty.[12]

Yes, all these years later, the New York Times discovers that President Bush was not lying when he said Saddam Hussein had Weapons of Mass Destruction. Not only were thousands of such weapons destroyed by the US Military during Bush's term, but many have been destroyed since Obama became president. I would say that he must have known about the WMDs once he became President but it always seems he gets his briefings by reading the papers (e.g. IRS Scandal, Obamacare Rollout Fumble, Jonathan Gruber, etc.).

President Bush crippled himself and his party by not disclosing this at the time. The constant refrain of "Bush lied, people died" was left unchallenged and it took hold. I have spent years saying we found chemical and biological weapons. It has been to no avail since I have changed no minds. The story that none were found sank into the consciousness of America and now, even after this revelation, I don't think that will change in my lifetime. It is too late. Much like Joe McCarthy has been tarred as a villain despite being proved correct in his claims of communists in the government, the WMD story will remain Bush lied.

Thursday, December 4, 2014

Unilateral Disarmament

You have to love the Republicans. They have just won a landslide victory for no other reason than they are not the Democrats. In that case, I suppose it would be more accurate to say the Democrats suffered a crushing defeat, a rejection of their policies that have given us an anemic economy and a pathetic world standing. Clearly, the voters want a change in direction. Therefore, before the new Republican majority takes office in a month, let's pass a budget that will last through September. What? Are you nuts? No, you are spineless Republicans.

Why would the Republicans allow the lame duck Democrat

Senate to be involved in a long term budget? It is not going to reflect Republican spending priorities. It isn't going to defund Obamacare. It will be a status quo ante budget that will take the power of the purse out of the incoming majority's hand until October. Why? First, fear of a shutdown. Yes, the Republicans are so terrified of a shutdown that they will do just about anything to avoid it, even if that makes the election meaningless. Obama knows this. He will veto the government into a shutdown and then blame Republican intransigence. That's what I would do! Duh! If the Republicans can't answer that, then the election is meaningless. Second, the Republicans want to spend the money. What is the point of taking over a multi-trillion dollar government and then reducing the amount of spending? Sure, that's what the voters want but they don't know how much fun it is to spend it and have people come on bended knee to beg for grants and tax exemptions.

It is funny that many Republicans have criticized Obama for taking military action off the table when negotiating with Iran, declaring that such can only embolden Iran and weaken our position. Are they oblivious to the parallels with government shutdown and impeachment? Never take it off the table unless you get something in return.

2015

More Doubts for Global Warming

I stumbled upon this interesting story:

The fiddling with temperature data is the biggest science scandal ever

New data shows that the "vanishing" of polar ice is not the result of runaway global warming

When future generations look back on the global-warming scare of the past 30 years, nothing will shock them more than the extent to which the official temperature records – on which the entire panic ultimately rested – were systematically "adjusted" to show the Earth as having warmed much more than the actual data justified.... [13]

Why would the data be adjusted? Who benefits? Government is funding this research because the results of the research are that we need to give government more money and more power. Governments aren't funding the 'climate deniers' because that isn't going to get more money and power for government.

Sunday, February 8, 2015

The Crusades

President Obama recently intimated that Christians had been very bad in the past and had no standing to condemn Islam today. He brought up the Crusades as an example. Let us consider that.

At the time of Muhammad's death in 632, Christianity was the dominant religion of the Mediterranean, including what is now Lebanon, Syria, Egypt, Algeria, Libya, Iraq, Jordan, Armenia, and Turkey. Then the Umayyad Caliphate arose. The caliphate spread through the region like wildfire, conquering all the Christian regions in the Levant, sweeping across North Africa, toppling the centuries old Visigoth Kingdom of Spain, and invading France. Not until Charles Martel defeated them at the Battle of Tours in 732 did the Islamic Conquest begin to recede. Christendom had been on the brink of being swept away. This was not because Muslim Imams had won hearts and minds with their preaching but because of fire and sword.

Europe was still mired in the Dark Ages and the Caliphate needed time to digest its conquests. The remains of the Roman Empire, known as the Byzantine Empire, fought an ongoing battle with Islam as it sought to gobble up more and more of Christian Anatolia (Turkey). Late in the 11th Century, the Byzantines requested aid from the West. Pope Urban II declared a Crusade in 1095. By 1099, Crusaders had recaptured a sliver of lands between Egypt and Anatolia. The vast majority of the territory that had been conquered in the 7th Century remained in the hands of the Fatimid Caliphate or the Seljuk Turks. By 1300, the Crusader States were gone. The Byzantine capitol of Constantinople finally fell in 1453. Greece and the Balkans fell also. In 1683, an Islamic army attacked Vienna, Austria.

The idea that the Crusades were an unprovoked attack is nonsense. The Crusades were a feeble response to centuries of Islamic attacks. Be it the various Caliphates, the Seljuk Turks, or the Ottoman Empire, Islamic states were at war with Christian states since the 7th Century. This remains true today though the tactics have changed.

While Jesus called upon his followers to turn the other cheek, Muhammad was a warlord who justified attacking caravans to gain wealth and power. This tells you most of what you need to know about both religions.

Thursday, February 26, 2015

Net Neutrality is what we had until today

"The government that governs least, governs best." Thomas Jefferson

Freedom is where there is unrestrained choice. Law exists to restrain some of those choices, such as murder and theft. Law provides a framework for a civil society but it also limits freedom. As such, one desires just enough law to maintain a civil society but not so much as to create a totalitarian regime. Lack of law leads to anarchy (e.g. Libya or Somalia) where excess of law leads to oppressive dictatorships (e.g. North Korea, Cuba).

The internet and the technology sector, which has existed mostly outside the bounds of government regulation, has been the most dynamic part of the economy. Coincidence? No. One does not put a pallet of bricks in the trunk of the car and then expect that to improve the acceleration. The same is true with government regulation. Regulations have both costs and benefits. The question should be asked if the benefits outweigh the costs. Government does not ask that question because the answer would lead to less regulation and therefore less government power. It is a rare person who voluntarily surrenders power. The regulations and the inevitably lawsuits they will trigger will send the internet into a decade of stagnation. There is no point investing when there is so much doubt about the future. Prices will rise and service will get worse.

On another point, has the government really demonstrated such good custodianship of late that it should be trusted to stick its fingers into another sector of the economy? How did that Stimulus fare? At the end of it, the president admitted that there had been no shovel-ready jobs after all. Nearly a trillion dollars of stimulus that was supposed to restore our ailing infrastructure and still the administration claims we have a crumbling infrastructure. Huh? Or how about the Affordable

Care Act? That is great, right? Keep your doctor, he said. Well, maybe not. Save $2500 per family, he said. Well, not so much. Costs went up instead. Maybe it has done better with foreign policy? No, it's one embarrassing mess after another. Yes, this is the government I want to entrust with policing the internet.

I am sure the regulations will be balanced, not weighing more heavily on those with views opposite the regulators (3 Democrats to 2 Republicans). You know, like the IRS jumped on MoveOn.Org just as much as various Tea Party groups. Oh, they didn't jump on MoveOn.Org? The regulators have used a 1930s law to regulate the internet. Maybe they should wait for Congress to pass a law? Really, shouldn't this be a decision by the elected representative of the people rather than a majority of 5 non-elective bureaucrats?

Saturday, February 28, 2015

IRS Emails Found!

"The IRS's inspector general confirmed Thursday it is conducting a criminal investigation into how Lois G. Lerner's emails disappeared, saying it took only two weeks for investigators to find hundreds of tapes the agency's chief had told Congress were irretrievably destroyed."[14]

Washington Times

Look, they found all those missing IRS emails. Despite the multiple crashed and trashed hard drives, the emails are still there. Wow! I don't work at the IRS and I knew the emails were still available. Somehow, the head of the IRS reported to Congress that the emails were lost. He claimed to have made much effort into retrieving the emails. Either he is abysmally ignorant of how email works or he was lying to Congress. The lowliest of lowly IT personnel at the IRS could have explained to Commissioner Koskinen that the emails were recoverable from offsite backups. Obviously, he didn't ask. Or, if he did, then he was clearly lying to Congress.

So why would he lie? If, as some have told me, the IRS was equally harsh against both conservative Tea Party groups and liberal groups, why try to cover up the evidence that must surely show exactly that? Obviously, it doesn't show that. It almost certainly shows that the IRS under the Obama Administration was used to harass enemies. If this same thing happened in a Republican administration, there would be demands to track this to its source. In fact, it would be assumed that the source was the Republican president and the media and the Democrats would be calling for impeachment.

Tuesday, June 2, 2015

I'm Batman!

If Bruce Jenner had come out and declared that he was actually Bruce Wayne, otherwise known as Batman, we would laugh. If he pressed the point too long, his family would seek psychiatric help. Instead, Bruce has declared that she is Caitlyn. That is laudable, even brave according to many.

Being inclined toward libertarianism, I am not bothered by Caitlyn's choice. It is her life. Live it how you wish to live it. What troubles me is the reaction of our culture to it. Norms are a thing of the past. Marriage shall be a compact of two (or more?) loving individuals. An English woman married a dolphin! Birth certificates will list parent 1 and parent 2 rather than mother and father. There are even calls to remove the baby's gender from the birth certificate. A tiny minority is not demanding just tolerance, but codification of its desires into the law. A dictatorship of the minority. To many, my failure to openly embrace this transformation of societal norms is akin to hate speech.

At this rate, what will be the cause in 20 years? What modern practice will turn out to be oppressive and discriminatory? What civil right yet remains?

Sunday, June 14, 2015

Warriors of the Wasteland

It is 2019 and the nuclear war that wiped out most of civilization was 9 years ago. Those who remain are either desperate refugees in search of some remaining pocket of civilization or the Templars. The Templars are a death cult who seek to exterminate survivors so that the earth will be purged of all humans. The Templars wear white and drive vehicles that look vaguely like moon buggies that are armed with ridiculous weapons. Being a death cult, there are no women among them and they are described as homosexuals. In fact, there is a sodomy scene in the movie!

Into the mix comes Scorpion, a former Templar who now roams the roads with no particular purpose beyond survival. Of course, he soon takes the side of the refugees and fights his former comrades. If not for the frequent intervention of Nadir the Archer, Scorpion would have been slain. Scorpion also has a mechanical prodigy as an ally. This blond 10 year old is not only a genius at customizing Scorpion's car but also an amazing combatant with a slingshot.

The movie is a bad *Road Warrior* knock-off. This is an Italian post-apocalyptic film with an all Italian cast except for Fred Williamson. Fred plays Nadir, an archer who fires explosive-tipped arrows. Guns are fairly common in the setting so it is unclear why he had decided to be an archer. Well, he does look cool. The car battles are a pale imitation of *Mad Max*.

Of note, I had seen a bit of this on late night TV 20 years ago and thought nothing of it. However, I recently saw *Mad Max: Fury Road* at the Alamo Drafthouse. The Drafthouse always has an applicable clip show before featured movie and it so happened that *Warriors of the Wasteland* (1983) was prominent. Well, I better check that out and write a review.

You Are What You Say You Are

On the heels of Bruce Jenner announcing that she is actually a woman named Caitlyn, we have Rachel Dolezal claiming to be black despite no black ancestors. However, Rachel does have a dash of Native American which is more than Elizabeth Warren or Ward Churchill can say. It is amazing how many whites want to claim membership in minority groups. Why? I thought whites had all the privileges. Well, sure, Ms. Warren was able to give herself a boost in getting hired by Harvard by being a minority but at what price? Now she is an Indian who is terribly repressed. She isn't? What of Rachel? Pictures of her in youth show a very white girl with blonde hair and freckles. As for Caitlyn, aren't white men at the top of the food chain? Why would anyone opt to be demoted to the less privileged sex?

Some of these people are gaming the affirmative action system that was put in place in the wake of civil rights movement of the 1960s. As for Rachel and Caitlyn, they are in denial. There are facts on the ground that they have both refused to accept. Our society has reached the point where it is wrong to correct them. That might be judgmental. It could hurt their feelings. A few years ago, Oregon declared a woman to be a man, which resulted in the pregnant man story. Well, he wasn't a man. He was a bearded lady but that would hurt his/her feelings. He/she wanted to be viewed as a man. Biology is no longer a valid basis for determining gender. Nor, it would seem, is it a valid basis for determining race. We have reached *1984* about 30 years after Orwell predicted. Male is female, white is black, surrender is victory.

Friday, June 26, 2015

Supreme Dork

Yesterday, the Supreme Court again ruled in favor of Obamacare. In his majority opinion, Chief Justice John Roberts ruled that

'Established by the State' does not necessarily mean 'Established by the State.' You see, that could ruin the law as it is currently being executed. Well, let's pause there. If the law is badly or ambiguously written, shouldn't it be returned to the Legislature to correct it? No, apparently not. Instead, the majority of the Court ruled that the law as the Obama administration has chosen to implement it (which has been modified from the law that the Supreme Court upheld in 2012) is just fine. Justice Scalia put it this way:

The Court's decision reflects the philosophy that judges should endure whatever interpretive distortions it takes in order to correct a supposed flaw in the statutory machinery. That philosophy ignores the American people's decision to give Congress '[a]ll legislative Powers' enumerated in the Constitution. Art. I, §1. They made Congress, not this Court, responsible for both making laws and mending them. This Court holds only the judicial power—the power to pronounce the law as Congress has enacted it. We lack the prerogative to repair laws that do not work out in practice, just as the people lack the ability to throw us out of office if they dislike the solutions we concoct. We must always remember, therefore, that '[o]ur task is to apply the text, not to improve upon it.'

The majority assumed the role of legislature and made the law conform to how the Executive Branch implemented it, not how the Congress (badly) wrote it.

Today, the Supreme Court ruled that gay marriage is Constitutional and must be allowed in all states, the democratic decisions of those states be damned. Chief Justice John Roberts, who yesterday was in favor of judicial legislation, wrote a strong dissent:

If you are among the many Americans—of whatever sexual orientation—who favor expanding same-sex marriage, by all means celebrate today's decision. Celebrate the achievement of a desired goal. Celebrate the opportunity for a new expression of commitment to a partner. Celebrate the availability of new benefits. But do not celebrate the Constitution. It had nothing to do with it.

Thus the Roberts' Judicial Doctrine is that 'legislating is acceptable when I am in the majority but a horrible breach when I am in the minority.' You can't have it both ways. Either you rule on the law as written or you don't. You can't pick and choose.

Friday, July 10, 2015

The Coming Mini Ice Age

Is a mini ICE AGE on the way? Scientists warn the sun will 'go to sleep' in 2030 and could cause temperatures to plummet

- *New study claims to have cracked predicting solar cycles*
- *Says that between 2030 and 2040 solar cycles will cancel each other out*
- *Could lead to 'Maunder minimum' effect that saw River Thames freeze over*

The Earth could be headed for a 'mini ice age' researchers have warned.

A new study claims to have cracked predicting solar cycles - and says that between 2020 and 2030 solar cycles will cancel each other out.

This, they say, will lead to a phenomenon known as the 'Maunder minimum' - which has previously been known as a mini ice age when it hit between 1646 and 1715, even causing London's River Thames to freeze over.[15]

So how do you feel about that 'Global Warming' now? Gee, maybe this explains the switch to Climate Change. I wonder how it will turn out to be our fault that the sun is going to sleep.

Saturday, July 25, 2015

Democratic Troubles

Democrats drop Thomas Jefferson and Andrew Jackson names from annual fundraising dinner

Thomas Jefferson and Andrew Jackson are history in Connecticut.

Under pressure from the NAACP, the state Democratic Party will scrub the names of the two presidents from its annual fundraising dinner because of their ties to slavery.

Party leaders voted unanimously Wednesday night in Hartford to rename the Jefferson Jackson Bailey dinner in the aftermath of last month's fatal shooting of nine worshipers at a historic black church in Charleston, S.C.[16]

The NAACP has demanded that the names of Thomas Jefferson and Andrew Jackson be dropped from an annual fundraiser because both men were slave owners. This does not bode well for the majority of former Democrat Presidents. Let's consider:

Thomas Jefferson (1801-09), the first Democratic-Republican president, was a slave owner. In fact, it is widely held that he had children with one of his slaves, Sally Hemmings.

James Madison (1809-17), Father of the Constitution, was a slave owner.

James Monroe (1817-25), Last of the Founding Fathers to serve as President, was a slave owner.

John Quincy Adams (1825-29) did not own slaves and was a noted Abolitionist, but he started as a Federalist and died as a Whig. If he had lived a few more years, he would have joined the Republican Party.

Andrew Jackson (1829-37), who founded the Democratic Party and was the 'jackass' that inspired the party symbol, was a slave owner.

Martin Van Buren (1837-41), called the Little Magician, was a New Yorker who thought slavery immoral, but it was Constitutional and beyond his authority. He only served one term and was not popular.

James Knox Polk (1845-49), the ultimate expression of America's Manifest Destiny, was a slave owner.

Franklin Pierce (1853-57) presided over Bleeding Kansas when he abandoned the Missouri Compromise, championed the Ostend Manifesto which was a secret effort to expand slavery to Cuba through purchase from Spain, and had Jefferson Davis as his Secretary of War. His is viewed as a failed presidency and he is often ranked as the worst President.

James Buchanan (1857-61) saw the Civil War coming and twiddled his thumbs. Regularly ranked among the worst presidents.

Grover Cleveland (1885-89; 1893-97) is the only Democrat elected president between 1861 and 1913. He is also the only one to server non-consecutive terms. Little remembered for anything else, he was not an enthusiastic supporter of the 15th Amendment (Votes for former slaves) and refused efforts to enforce their voting rights.

Woodrow Wilson (1913-21) was an apologist for the Ku Klux Klan. He was a segregationist and showed *Birth of a Nation* (1915) in the White House. On the other hand, he was in favor of the 19th Amendment (votes for women).

Franklin Delano Roosevelt (1933-45), who is regularly rated among the greatest presidents, setup internment camps for Japanese (George Takei being one of those interned as a child). He was also friendly with Joseph "Uncle Joe" Stalin, one of the greatest mass murderers in history. However, he was generally good to minorities (Japanese excluded), so the NAACP may not complain if his name is associated with a fundraising dinner.

Harry Truman (1945-53) presided over the Red Scare which he minimized but history has since shown that it was as bad as the much maligned Joe McCarthy said. Russia got the bomb and China went communist. Also, he approved the dropping of the bomb (I'm okay with that but most Democrats today are not). However, he is noted for desegregating the military and probably acceptable to the NAACP.

John F Kennedy (1961-63) allowed the FBI to tap Martin Luther King's phone. He also toppled the government in Vietnam that brought us fully into the war.

Lyndon Baines Johnson (1963-69) is generally viewed as a hero on Civil Rights grounds, but his presidency is tainted by Vietnam and urban riots. He continued the JFK policy of tapping MLK's phone.

Jimmy Carter (1977-81) is viewed as the worst president since Hoover. No one wants to have a fundraising dinner with his name on it. Who wants to revisit Iran Hostage Crisis right now?

William "Bill" Clinton (1993-2001) remains popular among his party despite having been impeached, having his law license revoked, and multiple affairs. Prior to President Obama, he had been called the 'First Black President.'

As many people have forgotten, the Democrats are the party of slavery and segregation. The NAACP will find that most Democrat presidents are unsuitable in today's climate. Maybe they should take a look at the Republican Party for a change.

War should be Hell

I recently watched the *Band of Brothers* miniseries from HBO. It came out a week before 9/11 and I saw a couple of episodes back then. It is an interesting show, more because of the contrast it provides with war today. The people who fought World War II have long been called The Greatest Generation and yet much of what they did would be considered war crimes under today's rules. World War II was fought to victory. We didn't have ceasefire agreements and peace talks. We fought until Germany and Japan surrendered unconditionally. How did that work out? Germany is the economic powerhouse of Europe and Japan has held that position in East Asia. Both are peaceful countries that haven't seen war since 1945. Gee, why don't we fight wars that way anymore?

First, we had another nuclear power on the scene. When the USSR became a nuclear power, it became necessary to prevent another total war. Thus, we held back in Korea and Vietnam, settling for a draw in the first and a loss in the second. With the fall of the Soviet Union, US power was supreme and yet, despite multiple conflicts, we still fought as if we feared escalation. Iraq cannot escalate. Afghanistan cannot escalate. There is no reason to fight a war of half measures. Or is there? In WWII, we flattened cities in Germany, Italy, and Japan. We bombed occupied ally cities. Civilian deaths were high. Such a strategy would be considered barbaric today. Pinpoint bombing has made war much more tolerable for civilians. Moreover, a reluctance to risk civilian casualties has provided enemies with a perfect shield; hide among civilians and Westerners won't shoot.

General Sherman said that 'War is Hell.' War should be Hell. War should be made as intolerable as possible so that it will end more quickly. All our civility has done is make it impossible to win wars. You want to end Islamic terrorism? Start flattening cities. Entire populations must be thoroughly convinced to abandon the current path. Moreover, any country that has any of this Islamofascism nonsense must be told in no uncertain terms to clean it up or the bombers will start appearing in their skies. If we fought WWII the way we are fighting the current War on Terror, we would have lost on both fronts.

Of course, it may be too late. Russia is on the rise. Is a new Soviet Empire being reborn? China is working on a navy to rival ours. The window of a single superpower is closing. In fact, it is closed for the foreseeable future since President Obama wants nothing more than to withdraw the US from the world. The consequences of that withdrawal are blooming.

Sunday, August 23, 2015

Dew Shine

It is well-known among my work colleagues that I drink Mountain Dew. My boss saw Dew Shine on a shelf and, not surprisingly, thought of me. I do like the presentation. My first thought was that it might be alcoholic. Apparently that is a common mistake; the label specifically states that it is not.

I found it to be more citrusy than standard Mountain Dew and possessed of an aftertaste almost as bad as Diet Mountain Dew. I'll keep the bottle as a souvenir but no more Dew Shine for me.

Crime? It Depends on Your Party-Affiliation

Remember the Valerie Plame fiasco during the Bush Administration? Richard Armitage had revealed Ms. Plame's name to Robert Novak. Novak mentioned it in a column and scandal ensued. Eventually, we had a Special Prosecutor to investigate this non-crime. Armitage was never charged with releasing Plame's name because she wasn't a covert agent: no crime. Still, it was a big deal and Scooter Libby - who did not reveal Plame's name to anyone - was convicted of a felony and fined $250,000.

Today, it is becoming increasingly clear that former Secretary of State Hillary Clinton had classified and top secret data on a private server located in a restroom closet in Denver. Some of these emails had to be copied from secure servers and transferred to Ms. Clinton's far less secure server. If someone of lesser status (or a Republican) had done this, there would be an immediate revocation of all security clearances and criminal charges filed. Thus far, nothing. Unlike Plame-Gate, crimes were clearly committed. Where is the Special Prosecutor?

Former Governor Rick Perry of Texas is currently under indictment (by a Democrat Prosecutor) for using his veto when he was governor. Apparently, using his veto - an integral power of his office - was a crime. This has surely contributed to his failing presidential campaign, which was the point.

Lois Lerner of the IRS somehow only allowed one conservative group to get tax-exempt status in the 3 years leading up to the 2012 election. When Congress sought to look into this anomaly, her emails from that window were reportedly destroyed in a hard drive crash. When asked to testify on the matter, she invoked her 5th Amendment privilege against self-incrimination. No charges have been brought against her or anyone at the IRS.

Tom DeLay, former Republican Congressman and very effective Majority Leader, was indicted (by a Democrat) for violating election laws. Because Republicans have standards, DeLay had to step down as majority leader while under indictment (Democrats have no such rules). He was eventually acquitted in the appeals court (8 - 1 ruling) but his political career was long over by then (again, that was the point).

Vice President Al Gore attended a fundraiser at a Buddhist Temple in California where thousands of dollars were funneled from China to the Clinton-Gore reelection campaign (that's a violation of election laws, by the way). Though some of the foreign fundraisers were charged and convicted, Janet Reno declined to appoint a Special Prosecutor to investigate the Clinton Administration's part in the crime.

A mere whiff of impropriety can torpedo a Republican but a city dump stench of scandal has little impact on Democrats. This double standard probably explains the spinelessness that I constantly attribute to Republicans. However, this is also why - even as a Libertarian - I prefer Republicans. The press will hammer them and the Democrats will oppose them tooth and nail. When Democrats are in office, the press cheers them and the Republicans are too scared to oppose them lest they be called racists, sexists, homophobes, or whatnot.

Saturday, August 29, 2015

Trump is a Symptom of Republican Spinelessness

Trump is Republican spinelessness come home to roost. Sure, he's not conservative and is only opportunistically a Republican but the man has spine. Both Republicans and Democrats have been telling the electorate how Amnesty/Path to Citizenship/ Legal Status for those who broke the law to get into the country is a *must*. Trump has thrown the BS Flag and he is suddenly in the lead for the Republican nomination. Gee, do you think maybe he has a better handle on the voters than the Washington elites? What is astonishing is that none of the other Republicans has tried to steal some of those voters by taking similar, if more nuanced, positions on illegal immigration. No, it isn't astonishing because they are spineless. Where most Republicans would apologize for having had the temerity to voice such a position and then slink away to obscurity, Trump added an exclamation point by having Jorge Ramos (a pro-illegal immigration propagandist from Univision) kicked out of a news conference. Trump is trying to win over voters, the rest of the Republican field is trying to win over a hostile media. Trump, like Gingrich in 2012, is thrilling primary voters by treating the media thusly. Trump is winning because he fights.

Let's contrast. The voters were clearly upset with Obama in 2010 and the Democrats were 'shellacked' in Obama's words. The Republicans took over the House, the part of the legislature with the power of the purse. Not one dime can be spent unless the House allows it. Obamacare was dead if only they had the spine to not fund it. Nope. No spine. Oh, they claimed that without the Senate, they were powerless. That's not what they said before the 2010 election. Fine. In the 2014 election, the Republicans won the Senate. No change. Now they claim that without the presidency, they can't do anything. Pathetic.

I'm no Trump fan but I wouldn't call him pathetic. I'd bet that if Trump had only one branch of the legislature, he would have accomplished vastly more than the 'professional' politicians. Of course, it might not be anything I want but he wouldn't be offering endless excuses as to why he wasn't delivering what he promised.

Sunday, August 30, 2015

The New Nobility

No Title of Nobility shall be granted by the United States
US Constitution, Article I, Section 9

Among those running for the Presidency are Hillary Clinton, the wife of former President Bill Clinton and Jeb Bush, son and sibling of two presidents (George Bush and George W. Bush). There is also Rand Paul, the son of long-serving Congressman Ron Paul and Lincoln Chafee, the son of life-long politician John Chafee. Lincoln actually inherited his father's Senate seat when the elder Chafee died. Oh, sure, the governor of Rhode Island 'appointed' him but that's pretty blatant. The United States should not have family dynasties in politics, especially at the national level.

To an extent, this is unavoidable. For millennia, most men found themselves in the same profession as their father. A farmer's son became a farmer, blacksmith's son a blacksmith, a cobbler's son a cobbler, and so forth. Even today, it is natural that a parent would impart knowledge of their chosen profession to their children. Many kids want to be like mom or dad. In most cases, that is fine. However, in politics, it is troublesome. With all the sway that former politicians accumulate (witness how many become lobbyists of their former colleagues), it creates dynastic families that are not so much elected as anointed. Would JEB Bush have done so well on fundraising if he weren't related to two former presidents? Would Hillary have been elected Senator in New York if she weren't married to the sitting president? Would either George W or Jeb have been elected governors of Texas and Florida if their father had not been president? For that matter, would George Bush have won a seat in congress in 1967 if not for his father, Senator Prescott Bush.

Family dynasties are incompatible with representative republics. When Jeb Bush announced his candidacy, he let it be known that he would seek the nomination without appealing to the Republican base. The base opposes Amnesty and Common Core; Bush favors both. If not for his family connections, he would already be toast. What of Hillary? Her campaign, such as it is, survives thanks to Bill's charm and popularity. Without Bill, Hillary would have had no political career at all.

Sadly, there is no legal fix for this. It would be inappropriate to deny people the opportunity to run for public office because a parent, sibling, or spouse had done so. The only solution is for the public to refuse to vote for them. I have not yet voted for a Bush or a Clinton and have no plans to ever do so. Please join me.

Tuesday, September 1, 2015

Safe House

I recently saw the 2013 movie and was less than impressed. The story opens with Tobin Frost (Denzel Washington) being pursued by unknown assailants in South Africa. He manages to escape into the US Embassy. It is here that we learn he is an infamous traitor who has sold US Intelligence secrets for a decade. A team is sent to interrogate him but they first transfer him to a safe house that is maintained by Matt Weston (Ryan Reynolds). Weston questions the legality of the interrogation when Frost is water boarded. The interrogation has hardly begun when the very assailants who chased Frost into the embassy attack the safe house. The interrogation team is all killed and it is left to Weston to escape with Frost and find another safe house. Of course, Frost is less than keen on resuming the interrogation at another site and escapes. Disgraced and his career likely over, Weston ignores orders to stand down and starts tracking Frost.

The movie is entertaining as it goes along. There are exciting action scenes, filled with instances where Weston and Frost become allies in the face of the unknown assailants and then enemies again. It doesn't take a rocket scientist to figure out that there is a mole in the CIA who leaked the location of the safe house. The movie offers several potential leakers though it is pretty obvious all along. And that leads to the moral of this movie: American Intelligence is evil and Tobin Frost was a hero for his treason. Yes, the traitor is the hero. And Matt Weston follows in his footsteps to become the new Tobin Frost.

Why must we have movies where the United States is the bad guy? Sure, I understood that Hollywood would have the US be bad guys during the Bush Administration; Hollywood is populated by Democrats. However, we've had Obama for years and still America is portrayed as bad and corrupt. The best thing that a patriot could do for the country is to commit treason. It sometimes appears that Hollywood is the propaganda arm of a hostile foreign power.

Saturday, September 5, 2015

Star Trek in Collapse

The Politics of Star Trek

From the New Frontier to the final frontier.

Leonard Nimoy's death in February brought to a close his unusual career continually playing a single role for half a century. Between 1966, when the television show Star Trek premiered, and 2013, when the movie Star Trek Into Darkness hit the screens, Nimoy portrayed the franchise's beloved first officer, Mr. Spock, in two TV series and eight films. As he acknowledged, the key to Star Trek's longevity and cultural penetration was its seriousness of purpose, originally inspired by creator Gene Roddenberry's science fiction vision. Modeled on Gulliver's Travels, the series was meant as an opportunity for social commentary, and it succeeded ingeniously, with episodes scripted by some of the era's finest science fiction writers. Yet the development of Star Trek's moral and political tone over 50 years also traces the strange decline of American liberalism since the Kennedy era.[17]

Timothy Sandefur's article delves into the changing morality of *Star Trek* from the Original Series in the 1960s, through the Next Generation, and up to the recent movie, *Star Trek Into Darkness*.

I was a huge fan of the original series. I loved Kirk, Spock, McCoy, Scotty, et al. So when The Next Generation arrived, I was excited. I watched the premiere and was not thrilled. I watched that first season and, though I could not effectively explain why, I didn't much like it. I was politically unaware at the time and the underlying philosophies of both the Original Series and The Next Generation didn't occur to me.

In my review of the latest Star Trek movie, I complained about the mindlessness of it but this article gets to the heart of the matter. It is interesting how Sandefur tracks liberal political ideology in a Sci-Fi TV/movie series.

Sunday, September 6, 2015

The Man from U.N.C.L.E

Our story opens with Napoleon Solo (Henry Cavill) crossing from West Berlin to East Berlin in 1963. He seeks to convince Gaby Teller (Alicia Vikander) to defect and help him locate her missing father, a Nazi scientist who had been working for the United States until his disappearance two years ago. Though she agrees, the pair are immediately pursued by Illya Kuryakin (Armie Hammer), a top KGB agent. The two prove well-matched but it is Solo who wins by getting Gaby to West Berlin. The following day, Solo and Kuryakin are shocked to discover that they have been made partners in order to prevent a nuclear weapon from being developed by a criminal organization. Gaby's missing father is believed to be involved, so Gaby will go with them to help ferret him out. The original series never explained how it was formed or the first meeting between Napoleon and Illya; this movie fills that gap.

I only saw one episode of the original series and it was nowhere near as funny as this. Solo and Kuryakin have a very adversarial relationship that provides many opportunities for laughs. However, as the movie progresses, the two clearly develop respect for each other. The movie often plays for laughs in other ways too. Solo is clearly the suave agent with gift for seduction and Gaby has already started to like him. Thus, it is funny when she is instead paired with Illya, who will play her fiancée. Illya is much less comfortable around women and such is played to the hilt with Gaby.

The movie ends with Alexander Waverley (Hugh Grant) of British Intelligence putting together a special team for a new agency, the United Network Command for Law and Enforcement (UNCLE). There is clearly room for a sequel. Though I liked the movie and give it a thumbs up, the box office looks insufficient to deserve a sequel.

Tuesday, September 8, 2015

Contempt for Thee but Not for Me

Kim Davis, the County Clerk of Rowan County, Kentucky, was sent to jail for contempt. She refused to issue marriage licenses to anyone in the wake of the Supreme Court decision that legalized gay marriage. She refused for religious reasons, though that is beside the point. It is also of note that she is a Democrat.

Meanwhile, throughout the rest of the country, various city officials have refused to report illegal immigrants to the Federal Government and openly declared themselves to be 'Sanctuary Cities' for these lawbreakers. Why have none of these officials been jailed for failing to follow the law? It is again of note that these officials are almost universally Democrats.

Of the two cases, Davis has better standing, at least from my perspective. Those who have established sanctuary cities are ignoring laws that were passed by congress and signed by the president. Ms. Davis is refusing to enforce a 'law' that congress did not pass. The lawmaking power is solely granted to the legislature, not the judiciary. Even if the congress had passed such a law and the president signed it, it would exceed the authority granted to the Federal Government by the Constitution. The only Constitutionally legal way to accomplish gay marriage would be to convince each state legislature to pass a law to that effect; such did not happen in Kentucky.

The rule of law is almost dead. President Obama has flouted the law repeatedly, as have many of his appointees (most obviously former Secretary of State Hillary Clinton). Laws that were passed are not enforced while laws that weren't passed are. Spineless Republicans have let it slide though they pretend they are doing something by having hearings that will result in no charges being filed. The Supreme Court has expanded its unconstitutional legislative role with Obergefell v. Hodges and

King v. Burwell; who needs Congress if the President and the Supreme Court can write and/or rewrite laws?

Wednesday, September 9, 2015

Gay Marriage Ratified in 1868!

Section 1. All persons born or naturalized in the United States, and subject to the jurisdiction thereof, are citizens of the United States and of the State wherein they reside. No State shall make or enforce any law which shall abridge the privileges or immunities of citizens of the United States; nor shall any State deprive any person of life, liberty, or property, without due process of law; nor deny to any person within its jurisdiction the equal protection of the laws.
14th Amendment of US Constitution

The men who wrote and ratified this amendment in 1868 would surely be surprised that they had codified abortion, anchor babies, and gay marriage. Their intent was to raise the freed slaves to full citizenship - which had been denied by Dred Scott - and force Southern States to treat them as equal to other citizens. Reading more into it than that is just judges stretching the law to allow them to rule whatever they want to rule. They aren't making new rights; they are merely adjudicating rights that have existed since 1868. Really?

There are two options: The amendment was intentionally written to achieve the modern ends or it was unwittingly written in a manner that allowed modern ends to be achieved. What is more likely? The answer is obvious. The amendment has too much wiggle room for 'interpretation' and the judiciary has exploited it. The judges on the Supreme Court all know the purpose of the amendment - they are lawyers who presumably made some study of the Constitution - but it provides endless power grab opportunities.

This is why original intent is so important. If you cut the Constitution free of the context in which it was written, much of the language suddenly becomes malleable to a variety of interpretations. Those who ratified the amendment in 1868 obviously didn't intend gay marriage to be validated. It isn't even arguable. But, having freed the amendment from its context, it is just a case of **equal protection** that allows a massive cultural shift that most states had voted against.

Thursday, September 10, 2015

The Uninformed Electorate

"Wherever the people are well informed they can be trusted with their own government."

Thomas Jefferson

I stumbled upon the following story today. It is not the first of its kind nor, sadly, will it be the last.

American adults get a D in science; 22% confuse astronomy and astrology

So says the Pew Research Center, which issued a report Thursday on the state of the nation's knowledge regarding some basic scientific facts.

The public opinion and research organization quizzed a representative sample of U.S. adults on geology, physics and astronomy, among other topics. Out of 12 questions, the test-takers answered 7.9 correctly, on average. That's a score of 66%.[18]

Here is yet more evidence that the American Electorate is not well informed. It is no wonder that so many accept Global Warming/Climate Change. Lacking any foundation upon which to judge claims, it quickly becomes impossible to make informed decisions. Last year, I posted a link to a YouTube video in which college students were quizzed about American government and politics; the results were disastrous.

When Davy Crockett returned to his district in Tennessee after a term in Congress, he had a farmer demanding for him to explain some of his votes and where the Constitution gave him the right to provide charity from the treasury. Here was an informed voter. Elected officials do not like informed voters because informed voters can hold them to account. On the other hand, uninformed voters will numbly nod to whatever a politician says:

"There's one issue that will define the contours of this century more dramatically than any other, and that is the urgent and growing threat of a changing climate."

Barack Obama, Sept 23, 2014

Plenty of skepticism has been published here regarding the Climate Change Hoax. It is a government power grab to get more taxpayer dollars and further limit freedom through 'common sense regulations.'

It is not by accident that our public education system is producing an uninformed electorate. That is its purpose. To whatever degree students are informed, it is indoctrination in favor of larger and more intrusive government. An armed (2nd Amendment) and informed (1st Amendment Freedom of the Press) electorate was meant to prevent the growth of over-reaching government.

"The natural progress of things is for liberty to yield and government to gain ground."

Thomas Jefferson

In the long game, it looks like the government is winning, just as Jefferson predicted.

Friday, September 11, 2015

Path to Defeat

Fourteen years after Pearl Harbor, World War II had been over for a decade. The Germans (the western half of them) and the Japanese were no longer a threat. Both were on a path to becoming powerful economies and much freer countries.

Fourteen years after 9/11, the War on Terror is still going

though it is mostly a loss. The costly victory of Iraq has been flushed away and now an Islamic State has arisen. The United States has approved a treaty that isn't a treaty with Iran that will remove sanctions and free billions of dollars in assets to a leading state-sponsor of terrorism. Does no one remember how well a far less generous nuclear deal with North Korea turned out? Europe is being flooded with waves of Muslim refugees who, strangely enough, are 70% adult males. Isn't it usually the women and children who flee while the men stay and fight? Millions of 'refugees' will soon be scattered throughout Europe and a percentage of those will prove to be ISIS agents out to cause mayhem. Heck, ISIS announced exactly that intention back in February. Our Middle Eastern allies, such as they were, in Iraq, Yemen, and Egypt have toppled or are in crisis. Libya, thanks to our intervention, went from a nominally stable dictatorship that was no longer a threat to a failed state crawling with Islamic fighters allied with al Qaeda. In short, the situation is much worse than when the war began. But Osama bin Laden is dead! Our current strategy is an obvious loser. It was weak under Bush and positively catastrophic under Obama.

During the Civil War, it took Lincoln years to find the right general. On paper, Grant didn't look as good as many of the generals who had preceded him but he proved to be the right man for the time. In the Cold War, it wasn't until Reagan that the right strategy was found against the Soviets. Once implemented, the Evil Empire collapsed surprisingly quickly. Obama may think the War on Terror has come to an end but the other side has not surrendered. They are ascendant. Will the next president be the right one to turn this war around? Not if she's Hillary. Hillary is one of the architects of the Libyan disaster. I've not heard any nominee correctly identify our enemy. Bush refused to do so and Obama had the Apology Tour during his first year in office.

Islam has been at war with the West for more than a thousand years. During that period, it has had its high points and low points but it never lost sight of the goal: subjugation of the world under an Islamic Caliphate. Thanks to the fecklessness of the West and a new strategy of stateless soldiers, Islam is making inroads. Everything we have done since 9/11 has had no impact on the enemy's resolve.

I fear it will require a radioactive smoking crater in place of a US city for us to finally take the enemy at their word and fight to victory.

Monday, September 14, 2015

The Confused Bernie Sanders

I hope that every person in this room today understands that it is unacceptable to judge people, discriminate against people based on the color of their skin. And I will also say, that as a nation — the truth is a nation that in many ways was created, and I'm sorry to have to say this from way back, on racist principles, that's a fact. We have come a long way as a nation. Now I know, my guess is that probably not everybody here is an admirer or a voter for Barack Obama, but the point is that in 2008, this country took a huge step forward in voting for a candidate based on his ideas and not the color of his skin.

Bernie Sanders

Gee, what are these racist founding principles?

We hold these truths to be self-evident, that all men are created equal, that they are endowed by their Creator with certain unalienable Rights, that among these are Life, Liberty and the Pursuit of Happiness

Declaration of Independence

That stands up just fine today and, I hope, Senator Sanders would agree. Did the United States live up to these principles? No, clearly not. In fact, it fell far short of the bar it set.

But the founding principles are as sound today as they were in 1776. Some might quibble about the use of 'men' rather than a neuter term, but it is otherwise unassailable. Though the country initially failed to live up to the principles that it championed, it eventually fought a Civil War that remains the bloodiest conflict in American history to rectify that. Even then, there was still much to do and, a hundred years after the Civil War ended, the Civil Rights movement swept away the state-sponsored discrimination that remained. That was fifty years ago. Since then, we have seen two black justices on the Supreme Court, two black Secretaries of State, a black Attorney General, and President Barack Obama. Sounds like the country finally arrived at the goal it stated almost 250 years ago. In short, the principles were just fine, it was the implementation of them that was a problem.

Also, Barack Obama was elected not for his ideas - which were massively rejected in the 2010 'shellacking' election, but because he was black. A white candidate with the same ideas would have been trounced (e.g. George McGovern, Michael Dukakis, et al). Many hoped that electing a black man as president would finally put an end to Racist America. Really, how can the country be racist if it elects a black man? Instead, thanks to Obama himself, it got worse but that's a blog for another day.

Tuesday, September 15, 2015

A Right to be Believed?

I want to send a message to every survivor of sexual assault. Don't let anyone silence your voice. You have a right to be heard. You have a right to be believed. We're with you.

Hillary Clinton

Taking on her words, I have a couple of instances I would like to address during her next press conference?

Juanita Broaddrick alleged that Attorney General Bill Clinton raped her in 1978, leaving her with a swollen lip and torn pantyhose. Should her voice have been silenced? Did you believe her?

Paula Jones revealed that, in 1991, then Governor Bill Clinton had arranged for her to meet him at a Little Rock hotel where he exposed himself and suggested she 'kiss it.' Did she have a right to be believed?

Kathleen Willey said that President Bill Clinton sexually assaulted her in 1993; did she have a right to be believed?

During your husband's political career, you referred to such incidents at 'bimbo eruptions' and set about denying them. It was all part of a 'vast rightwing conspiracy,' you said. Republicans must have sneaked Monica Lewinsky into the Oval Office and thus entrapped President Clinton. He sat beside you during a *60 Minutes* interview and denied any relationship with Gennifer Flowers only to be exposed as a liar soon thereafter when Flowers offered an incriminating audio cassette. Monica Lewinsky likewise was able to provide irrefutable evidence of an adulterous relationship with President Clinton; should you have believed her?

With her history, this is a subject that Hillary shouldn't touch with a 10 foot pole. She spent much too long trying to silence and discredit women who offered tales of sexual assault to now switch sides.

On the other hand, even a person with a problematic history on a subject could come to the truth. Witness Paul's conversion on the road to Damascus. But that is not the case here. We have had too many false accusations of late (Duke Lacrosse Team, Rolling Stone UVA gang rape story, Mattress Girl at Columbia, Lena Dunham's Oberlin College rape story, etc.) to offer a blanket right to be believed. Rape and sexual assault are crimes. The accused needs to be tried in a court of law, not a court of public opinion. Even as heinous as the crime is, the accused is still presumed innocent. Representative Jared Polis (D-CO) should be censured by his colleagues for his suggestion that the innocent should be expelled along with the guilty, just to make sure.

Importing Voters

With about 8.8 million legal residents in the country who are eligible to become citizens, White House officials said they were trying to make it easier to complete the final steps to citizenship.

The officials said they had started the campaign this week because Thursday is Citizenship Day. But the White House is also aware of federal figures showing that about 60 percent of immigrants eligible to naturalize are Latino and about 20 percent are Asian, both groups that voted overwhelmingly for President Obama. Nearly a third of legal permanent residents eligible to naturalize are Mexican.

New York Times

Why try to convince the citizens that your prescriptions for the nation are best when you could just import more voters who are inclined to your viewpoint? This is why the Democrats are not at all troubled by illegal immigration. Look what happened to California. Here was a state that was regularly electing Republican governors and was often in the Republican column in presidential elections. Now the state doesn't have a single Republican in statewide office and it is in the Democrat column of every presidential election.

From 1820 to 1960, 80% of all immigrants came from Europe. The majority of them were from Germany, Ireland, Italy, and the UK. Only 14% came from the Americas, the vast majority of those from Canada. Only 3% of all migrants from 1820 to 1960 were from Mexico. Also during that 140 year period, only 3% of migrants were from Asia.

From 1960 to 1990, the pattern was turned on its head. Europe only accounted for 17% of all migrants in that period. Asia rocketed to 32% of all migrants while the Americas now accounted for 48% of immigrants. No longer were Canadians the biggest portion of that group; Mexico took the top spot, providing 4 times as many immigrants as Canada. In fact, Mexico alone accounted for more immigrants (2.7 million) than all of Europe (2.6 million).

This shift in American immigration was not by chance. As noted by the New York Times, Latinos are more likely to vote Democrat. The more Latinos that can be imported and made voters, the better the election returns are for the Democrats. Again, witness California. From 1952 to 1988, California voted Republican for President in all but 1 election. From 1992 to present, it has gone Democrat. It is no coincidence that this shift occurred after Reagan had signed an Amnesty in 1986 with promises of border security and immigration enforcement that have worked out SO well.

In much the same way that Europe is transforming into Eurostan thanks to a huge influx of Muslim immigrants who are far more fertile than the native populations, the United States is on a similar path of transformation by a different set of migrants who are more fertile. If a nation doesn't control its borders, it ceases to be a nation. The elites who live in gated communities are sadly indifferent to cultural shifts brought about by such uncontrolled immigration.

The voters understand this. It is why they crushed George W. Bush's Comprehensive Immigration Reform Act (i.e. Amnesty) in 2007. It is why Trump, who founded his campaign on opposition to illegal immigration, is so dominant. The legal immigration is bad enough, why exacerbate it with illegal immigration?

Saturday, September 19, 2015

Democrat Debate

There has been much grief from lesser candidates in the Democrat field that there are only going to be 6 debates. There are 19 declared candidates though I doubt most Democrat voters could name more than 3. Of course, only the top five are of note:

Hillary Clinton

Former Secretary of State, New York Senator, First Lady. She is the current front runner. Her email scandal is damaging her standing. On account of this, the top three words associated with her in a Quinnipiac poll were "liar," "dishonest," and "untrustworthy." She has more than a year to counter that but the continued bleeding and lack of resolution with the email server will be an anchor on her campaign. She is a member of the New Nobility.

Bernie Sanders

Vermont Senator, former Congressman & Mayor of Burlington. He is a self-described socialist and Clinton's most successful rival at this point. Bernie is an Independent who caucuses with the Democrats in the Senate. Unlike Democrats who only offer lip service to opposing Wall Street (while taking the lion's share of political donations from them), Bernie is a true believer. As such, the party elites do not want him.

Martin O'Malley

Former Maryland Governor and Baltimore Mayor. He barely registers in the polls at this point, thus his strong interest in lots of debates. He is likely hamstrung by the failure of his hand-picked successor to win the governorship. Also, the recent trouble in Baltimore reflects on him, fairly or not. However, he is a solid Democrat with executive experience who doesn't have the baggage of Hillary or the outspoken socialism of Bernie.

Jim Webb

Former Virginia Senator and Secretary of the Navy. He served in the Reagan administration and is too pro-military and bipartisan to win the Democratic nomination. The most conservative of this leftist field, he is going nowhere.

Lincoln Chafee

Former Rhode Island Governor, Senator, Mayor of Warwick.

Former Republican, former Independent. Lincoln was a liberal Republican back when that was openly allowed. He has since transitioned to a Democrat. He wants to US to switch to the Metric System. He is a member of the New Nobility.

The choice of the party elites is clearly Hillary, thus the desire for as few debates as possible. Hillary lacks her husband's charm and political instincts; thus debates are likely to harm her candidacy while offering alternatives. The last time the voters were given an alternative to Hillary, they took him.

Of late, there has been a growing 'Draft Biden' movement that would like to see Vice President Joe Biden jump into the race. For the political novice, this might sound like a great idea but Biden has plenty of baggage himself, from plagiarism to inaccurately reporting his voting record on issues like Iraq. This is a man who lost the nomination to Dukakis in 1988.

There is also some hope that, if Hillary falters, Elizabeth Warren might jump into the race. Warren is quite popular with the base, probably more so than Hillary. This popularity with the base is unlikely to translate to the general election voter. I see her as the counterpart of Ann Coulter; Coulter is hugely popular with the base but couldn't possibly hope to get elected because of her divisive nature. Warren has had electoral success in the bluest of blue states. Let's see, how did Dukakis do on the national scene?

Obviously, I am opposed to all of these candidates but with no incumbent, it does strike me as fair to have lots of debates to give the voters an opportunity to get to know the candidates. The Republicans have already had two debates, the second of which has so far been great for Carly Fiorina. O'Malley, Webb, and Chafee certainly wish they had such an opportunity to connect with the voters. They should get it and the base agrees.[19]

Friday, September 25, 2015

Boehner Resigns at Last!

John Boehner, Republican Speaker of the House, has announced that he is resigning. He will remain in position for 1 month, long enough to cave-in to Obama's budget demands on Planned Parenthood. Yes, with nothing to lose, Boehner is almost certainly going to leave office in much the same way he served, spinelessly.

When Boehner first became Speaker in 2010, I was optimistic that the Republicans might push back against the leftism of the president. Time and again, he demonstrated an unwillingness to fight for Republican principles, or any principles. Now and again, he would talk a good game but he never enacted it. No, for four years, all I heard from him was that he could not stop the president's agenda unless Republicans won the Senate. Then came the 2014 election in which the Republicans crushed the Democrats, acquiring the Senate. Finally, the Republicans will stand against the leftism of the president. No, instead they passed a budget that would constrain the Power of the Purse for the incoming majority. They didn't want to risk a shutdown so soon after such landslide election. Um, why do you think the voters chose you, the opposition party, if not to oppose?

When the Republicans won their sweeping victory in the 2014 election, I was sadly correct in my prediction of the difference it would make: none. The Republicans have failed their voters to such a degree that the voters will follow anyone who seems to have a spine. Donald Trump has a spine. Four years of Boehner's feckless leadership has brought the Republican party to this sad state. Boehner has secured for himself a failed Speakership, an example of what not to do for future Speakers.

The current expectation is for the Majority Leader, Kevin McCarthy, to be the next speaker. If he is, the Republicans will demonstrate that they haven't learned their lesson. Why have one milquetoast resign to be replaced by another. That may be unfair to McCarthy but I had no idea who he was until today. That he has been the majority leader for this disaster of a

Congress is not a good sign.

Now if only Mitch McConnell would resign from the Senate...

Saturday, September 26, 2015

Truth according to Hollywood

In 2004, Dan Rather broke a story on 60 Minutes that claimed George W. Bush had gone AWOL from his National Guard Unit. The story fell apart almost immediately when bloggers were able to reproduce identical copies of the documents in Microsoft Word. It was obvious that the documents had not been created on a 1960s typewriter but on a 2004 computer. As the story came crashing down, it came out that the 60 Minutes producer of the story, Mary Mapes, had contacted the Kerry campaign and offered her source to it; this was not the action of a disinterested reported but rather a partisan hack. Mapes was fired in the wake of the story and Dan Rather's career ended shortly thereafter. Even so, both Rather and Mapes asserted that the story was true even if the documents were forgeries.

Next month, Robert Redford will portray Dan Rather and Cate Blanchet will be Mary Mapes in the movie adaptation of Mapes memoir on the subject. Rather has seen the film and was quite pleased. Between the fact that it is based on Mapes' memoir and Rather's glowing review, how accurately might it reflect my thumbnail sketch? I bet the collusion between Mapes and the Kerry Campaign won't appear in the film. It will probably re-litigate the AWOL Bush story, again claiming the story is true despite the falsity of the documents that 'prove' it. Mapes and Rather will be shown as heroes and the bloggers who exposed their specious story the villains.

What this means is that it is okay for the media to lie and fabricate as long as it is for a good cause, such as opposing the election of a Republican. To apologize for having to fire her - for cause, no less - the liberal establishment will now lionize her. How many who were too young or politically unaware in 2004 will swallow Mapes' retelling whole? Hollywood has a habit of making these revisionist or selective history movies that invariably reflect well on Democrats and badly on Republicans.

Sunday, September 27, 2015

Republican Turmoil

What is going on in the Republican Party? For many years, the party has been split in two general groups: The Establishment and the Conservatives. The Establishment - which includes retiring Speaker John Boehner and Senate Majority Leader Mitch McConnell - are fairly content with the current size of government so long as they get to drive the car. Right now, the car is a Ferrari La Ferrari (the most expensive sports car on the market at $1.4 million) and the establishment members love it. They don't admit they love it. They talk about wanting to pare down the government but that Ferrari is just so much fun to drive. The conservative wing of the party thinks the Ferrari is too expensive. Those of a more Libertarian bent would opt for a Toyota Camry, which is plenty robust if the government keeps within its Constitutional limits. The majority of the conservatives - Tea Party Caucus - would be content to just have a Lamborghini. Sure, it's still a ridiculously expensive car ($540K), but much more economical than the current Ferrari.

The problem for the Establishment wing of the party is that the primary voters are predominantly conservatives and taxpayers. These voters are paying for the government to have a Ferrari while they are stuck driving a Ford Fiesta. They have repeatedly listened to the establishment and chosen 'electable' candidates like Dole, McCain, and Romney only to discover they weren't electable after all. No one wants to sacrifice their values to back a loser. Even when they won with George W Bush, they lost. The government got bigger, a new entitlement (Drug Benefit) and a cabinet department (Homeland Security) were created. The spinelessness of the Republicans to oppose Obama's agenda despite having both houses of Congress has been the last straw.

This is why the top three candidates in the race have no elective experience.

Of course, the Democrats aren't happy with the Ferrari either. They want another one.

Monday, September 28, 2015

Trump's Tax Proposal

Income Tax Rate	Long Term Cap Gains/ Dividends Rate	Single Filers	Married Filers	Heads of Household
0%	0%	$0 to $25,000	$0 to $50,000	$0 to $37,500
10%	0%	$25,001 to $50,000	$50,001 to $100,000	$37,501 to $75,000
20%	15%	$50,001 to $150,000	$100,001 to $300,000	$75,001 to $225,000
25%	20%	$150,001 and up	$300,001 and up	$225,001 and up

These are the Trump rates, simplifying our current system of 7 brackets down to 4 brackets and doing away with many of the deductions, sort of a Reagan redux but less ambitious; Reagan's tax reform left us with 2 brackets. Also, he plans to close loopholes and stick it to the hedge fund managers. I like simplicity in the tax code.

As someone who would love nothing more than to abolish the IRS and repeal the 16th Amendment to the Constitution (the one that provides for an income tax), it will come as a surprise that I don't like the 0% bracket. Everyone should pay some tax. Of course, that is a political loser since so many people are already in the 0% bracket in the current tax system. Yes, that is a bad thing. If someone pays no income tax, he has no incentive to keep taxes from rising. In fact, there is an incentive to have taxes on others rise in order that those not paying taxes can receive more generous government benefits.

Though my econ classes taught that an old tax is a good tax (because the market has already adapted to it), I disagree. Income tax requires that the government know everyone's income. What business is it of government how much a person makes? What happened to that right to privacy? It requires a massive and, as recent events have shown, corruptible bureaucracy. This is why a national sales tax is preferable. It taxes consumption, which will have the benefit of encouraging saving. Much as state sales taxes exempt food items, a national sales tax could do the same. The rich will pay much more because they will consume much more. Better still, the government need not know how much anyone earns and no one need ever file a tax return. Furthermore, Congress wouldn't be able to pit the rich against the poor against the middle class. The very best of all would be the visibility of it on every transaction by every taxpayer; no more withholding that hides the cost of government; if it goes up a penny, everyone will know and want an explanation. Yes, the tax accountants would hate it and I am sure they are even now lobbying against such a wicked idea. Such a system would take too much power away from politicians so they will never willingly allow it to pass.

Trump's plan is better than what we have but not as good as Rand Paul's. He would have a single tax rate of 14.5% with certain deductions. This would be for everything. Now that is simplicity. The economy would love it though Congress would, as aforementioned, be apoplectic about the loss of power. As stated in another blog, the tax code is a protection racket where the Congress provides special tax breaks to certain donors and lobbyists. This is why the codes keeps getting convoluted and colossal. So long as the 16th Amendment exists, that will forever be the case.

Tuesday, September 29, 2015

The End of Pax Americana

In the Ancient World, there was a period that has come to be called the Pax Romana, the Roman Peace. After two centuries of almost continuous warfare, Augustus brought about an era of peace in the wake of his victory over Antony and Cleopatra. This extended period of no warfare was unknown to Romans but not unwelcome. It lasted for two hundred years but came to an end with Commodus (Joaquin Phoenix in Gladiator).

Based on this Roman example, historians have picked out other similar time and titled them for the dominant power that secured the peace. After Napoleon's final defeat at Waterloo, Britain became the dominant power around the globe. Its mighty navy protected the seas and thereby promoted trade and comity on the waves. This Pax Britannica lasted until World War I. It was not until after World War II that the United States took the reins from Britain and established the Pax Americana. Of course, there have been wars during this period but they have not touched the American mainland - terrorist attacks excepted.

Barack Obama has refused to maintain the Pax Americana. From the very start, he apologized for America's past arrogance and declared that we had no business telling other countries what they should and shouldn't do. He abandoned allies like Poland to curry favor with opponents like Russia. He abandoned Iraq and is somehow bemused that ISIS arose in the fertile power vacuum he left. He was a cheerleader for the Arab Spring which has toppled our former allies - though admittedly dictators - and provided more fertile soil for jihadists; that was not a good tradeoff. The Middle East is in ruins and expelling refugees at an alarming rate. Iran is on the rise and aligning itself with Russia. Russia has become a firm supporter of Assad in Syria, a dictator that Obama long ago demanded step down. Russia, whom Romney identified as our number one geopolitical adversary in the 2012 campaign, is securing a foothold in the Middle East while we retreat from it.

As happened with the Pax Britannica, America is finding it more difficult to pay for the peace. With an economy that has stagnated for the better part of a decade and a rapidly growing welfare state to support, it is easier to cut the military than transfer payments to voters.

At the UN today, Vladimir Putin laid the blame for Middle

Eastern turmoil on the West. And he was right! Obama has left a power vacuum and Putin is only too happy to accept this gift. During the Cold War, we funded the Mujahidin in Afghanistan, a country with relatively little in the way of natural resources. Now we are handing over the whole of the Middle East, a magnificent oil producer, without resistance.

I rather doubt we will have a Pax Russia to follow America's abdication.

Thursday, October 1, 2015

Foreign Policy Collapse

As a world power, the United States has vanished. The Obama Presidency has marched the country off a cliff. There are no successes, only degrees of failure.

From Tunisia to Iran, there is a string of foreign policy disasters, many of which can be laid on the front runner for the Democratic nomination, Hillary Clinton. Libya is a mess and Secretary Clinton proudly proclaimed, "We came, we saw, he died." Looking at it now, one has to agree that we were better off with Ghaddafi. Iran, who was still having weekly 'Death to America' rallies throughout the negotiations on the 'Nuclear Deal,' is having sanctions lifted and assets unfrozen in exchange for... nothing. Nope, the only thing we get out of it is a piece of paper that says we have a deal. It might win a Nobel Peace Prize for John Kerry. With Russian planes now stationed in Syria and warships in its harbors, Assad is certain to survive. Russia commenced bombing but didn't target ISIS. No, they bombed the rebels that we are supporting, the ones that were fighting Assad. All that 'red line' and 'wrong side of history' talk amounts to nothing. Egypt? Military dictatorship not unlike that of Mubarak but much less friendly to the US. Yemen? Only a few months after Obama declared it a model for US foreign policy, it collapsed. Afghanistan? We are only still there because Obama had called it the 'right war' so that he could fustigate

Bush about the wrong war in Iraq.

China is on the rise both in Asia and Latin America. As it is building a military at a rapid rate, the US has weakened itself economically and militarily in relation. Japan is sufficiently alarmed that it is altering the rules for its Self-Defense Force. The American shield that Japan relied upon for the last 60 years no longer inspires the confidence it once did.

Europe is at threat of being squeezed by an ascendant Russia. Russia already controls the majority of natural gas that goes to Europe. With its moves in the Middle East (Syria, Iran, Iraq) combined with its own considerable petroleum reserves, it may eventually have a chokehold on European energy. That the US is barred from exporting oil only exacerbates the problem. Russia has already annexed portions of Georgia and Ukraine and is pushing for more. Right out the gate, Obama has encouraged such adventurism on Putin's part by nixing the missile defense deal we had with Poland and the Czech Republic. Hillary Clinton's childish reset button showed them how unserious we were. Then Obama moved into full surrender mode with his announcement that he would be 'more flexible' after the 2012 election. We are seeing just how flexible.

Not resting on these failures, Obama pushed on to surrender to Cuba. Yes, after more than 50 years, we finally recognized the Castro brothers. No demands on human rights were made or return of property in order to gain diplomatic recognition. Fidel can now die knowing that he brought America to heel.

Is it possible that the policy makers in Washington are this incompetent? Can such a dramatic and overwhelming collapse be an accident or did we finally elect the Manchurian Candidate? That sounds like tinfoil hat conspiracy stuff to me but the evidence is damning. Of course, Obama did tell us that he didn't like America as the sole superpower and declared that he was a 'citizen of the world' when he was running for President of the

United States. Maybe we should have taken him on his word.

Friday, October 2, 2015

Government is the Most Dangerous Mass Murderer

Yet another crazy has gone on a shooting spree in a gun free zone and there are immediately calls for gun control. Yes, gun control has done wonders for Chicago, New York, and Washington DC. Let's bring that same gun murder rate to the rest of the country. The Second Amendment guarantees the right of the people to bear arms because the people have a right to defend themselves. That right was denied to certain groups in the 20th century and it didn't turn out well.

In 1911, the Ottoman Empire banned guns. A few years later, a million and a half Armenians were murdered. The Soviet Union banned guns in 1929. The following decade, millions of Ukrainian Kulaks were murdered through mass starvation. Dissident Russians found themselves sent to Siberian gulags. In 1938, Germany banned guns. Shortly thereafter, millions of Jews were shipped off to death camps. Where the Jews managed to have weapons, there were uprisings, the most famous of which was the Warsaw Ghetto Uprising in 1943. China had banned guns in the 1930s, just in time for the Japanese invasion. Oddly, the ban was still in effect after the war and during the rule of Mao Zedong. Up to 50 million Chinese were killed during Mao's Cultural Revolution. Cambodia instituted total gun control in 1956. When Pol Pot seized power two decades later, he exterminated 2 million unarmed Cambodians, a quarter of the country's population. Cuba, North Korea, and Iran do not allow private citizens to have guns.

This is not to say that gun control automatically leads to mass murder by the government. Both the United Kingdom and Japan have very strict gun control but it is unlikely that a government will arise in either that would murder its citizens. But if one did, the people would be helpless to resist. And that is why we have the 2nd Amendment. Yes, there are costs to such liberal gun laws. These costs are only made worse by gun free zones. The way to stop a bad guy with a gun is for a good guy with a gun to arrive on scene. All those law-abiding citizens are necessarily disarmed while law is no impediment to the shooter.

Today's government might want to take your gun for what it views as good and rational reason. It will do you no harm and in fact only have your best interest at heart. However, tomorrow's government - perhaps 20 years from now - might look upon you as a nuisance that has no means to resist its will.

Saturday, October 3, 2015

Willful Blindness, Literally!

I read the most unusual headline:

Woman Fulfills Lifelong Wish To Be Blind, Now Happier Than Ever

This I have to read. It turns out that Jewel Shuping has long thought she was meant to be blind and finally set about making herself so. The woman had Body Integrity Identity Disorder (BIID), which is usually associated with people who want to amputate limbs. I say had because she seems to have 'cured' herself by actually becoming blind. How did she become blind? The story tells us.

In 2006, Shuping found a psychologist who was willing to help her become blind. The psychologist began putting numbing drops in her eyes, followed by a couple of drops of drain cleaner.

Amazingly, the story doesn't discuss criminal charges against this psychologist, the revocation of a license to practice psychology, question this person's ethics, or anything along those lines. No, nothing more is said about the psychologist.

"I really feel this is the way I was supposed to be born, that I should have been blind from birth, When there's nobody around you who

feels the same way, you start to think that you're crazy. But I don't think I'm crazy, I just have a disorder."[20]

Yes, she is crazy and the psychologist assisted her in her craziness. It is a **dis**order, right?

If you want to be blind, poke your eyes, pour Drano on your eyes, or whatever, but the idea of a medical practitioner assisting in this endeavor really troubles me. What happened to *First, do no harm*? This is the same reason I am opposed to doctor-assisted suicide. You aren't all that eager to die if you need someone present to assist.

If all that wasn't bad enough, the tone of the story is positive. Look at the headline! The reporter is all-in on the goal of blindness. The only disapproval comes in the off-handed line that Shuping's mother and sister are no longer on speaking terms with her. Can you believe that she has such an unsupportive family? What does it say about American culture that the story was covered this way?

Sunday, October 4, 2015

Olympus Has Fallen

One of two movies to premiere in 2013 with the premise of the White House being captured by terrorists, I found it generally disappointing though not as far-fetched as such an idea should be. The fact that a lone man jumped the fence and got into the White House last year makes this much more plausible.

The movie supposes an impossible attack on the White House occurs. An enemy airplane briefly dominates the Washington DC airspace and strafes the White House, killing most of the defensive forces on the roof and many on the ground. Then a ground assault takes place with forty men with automatic weapons charging across the south lawn while being supported by 50 caliber emplacements from the street. RPGs and suicide vests are used to breach fences and doorways. Meanwhile, the President has retreated to his bunker, taking the South Korean Premier and his entourage with him. Not surprisingly, the premier's security team are all plants and quickly subdue everyone in the bunker; Olympus has fallen.

The president (Aaron Eckhart) demonstrates repeated bad judgment that leads to a near catastrophe for the country at the end. He ordered that the South Korean security team be included in the bunker despite a protest from a Secret Service agent. He ordered the Joint Chiefs of Staff to reveal a top secret code, since it was useless without the other two codes. Then he ordered his Secretary of Defense to reveal the second code, since it was useless without the other code. Then the enemy hacker broke the third code. Who saw that coming? But it gets worse.

The military has finally arrived on scene only a couple of minutes after the last Secret Service agent died in the White House and signaled, "Olympus has fallen." Do they charge in to retake the place? No, the bad guy tells them to stand down or he will start killing hostages. The President, in a rare moment of good judgment, said," Don't negotiate" before he was shoved out of the camera. General Clegg (Robert Forster) did not negotiate; he immediately acceded to the terrorist's demands. He stood down his forces on the scene and allowed the terrorists to secure the perimeter and put together an anti-air defense system. Speaker Trumbull (Morgan Freeman) arrives at the Pentagon to learn he is the acting president. He also decides not to attack the White House and even complies with the terrorist demands that the 7th Fleet be withdrawn from the Sea of Japan and that US troops withdraw from South Korea. He knows this will likely result in a war that will cost thousands upon thousands of lives but, in order to save a few hostages in the president's bunker, he does it anyway. By their decisions, President Asher, General Clegg, and Acting-President Trumbull allow the terrorists to nearly achieve a national apocalypse. Why didn't they resist? To save a dozen hostages. Only 2 hostages survived with their chosen path.

Of course, much of this happens on the fringe of the main story which follows Secret Service Agent Mike Banning (Gerard Butler) stalking about the ruins of the White House and, *Die Hard* style, killing off the terrorists. That part was a lot of fun with guns, knives, and fisticuffs galore.

Again, the very premise of the movie is ludicrous. Such an attack could not have hoped to succeed. The enemy aircraft would not have been able to dispatch the US interceptors and the Secret Service agents at the White House would not have stood on the lawn armed only with pistols like shooting ducks. But if it did happen this way, the President would be impeached when it came to light that he ordered the release of codes and that he broke protocol to allow the terrorists into his bunker. General Clegg was in a hard situation with the civilian chain-of-command broken and might have felt an assault on the White House wasn't his decision to make (if only the president had said "attack" instead of "don't negotiate"). Even so, he would likely lose his job in the aftermath. Speaker Trumbull was Acting President. He did not act in the interest of the country but in the interest of a dozen hostages in the president's bunker. He does not deserve a leadership position. I guess that part didn't make it into the movie. Maybe in the sequel.

White House Down

Having just watched *Olympus Has Fallen*, I decided to watch its competitor. The events are surprisingly similar - not only do we have another president held hostage in the White House, we have a Speaker of the House become President. However, this one is extremely political. Whereas I did not know the party affiliation of the characters in Olympus, that is not the case here. President Sawyer (Jamie Foxx) is a thinly veiled Barack Obama. Really, the guy wants to pull troops out of the Middle East and is having high level talks with Iran! The Speaker of the House is a wicked evil traitor who is in the pocket of the military industrial complex; his first order of business is to keep US troops in the Middle East. Of course, President Sawyer's plan to withdraw all US forces from the Middle East is declared a success in the film's epilogue, with both Iran and Israel jumping eagerly at the opportunity. All you need to do is give peace a chance.

Thanks to high-level traitors in the government, this White House take-over comes across as less ludicrous. Agent Walker (James Woods), head of the Secret Service in the White House, would have the best chance of sneaking a special ops team into the White House. Such a command position allowed him to undermine a proper response - misdirecting responders - so long as he was still viewed as loyal. However, it seems highly unlikely that a man whose son was killed on an operation ordered by the president would retain that position.

The action was great and it was funny to see the buddy cop vibe between the president and John Cale (Channing Tatum). There was a surprising amount of comedy in the movie. The President switching to sneakers in the residence, a villain putting a call on hold, the Vice President's aide hanging up on the president's call, and even the White House Tour Guide was funny: "Tour's over." If not for the overt political message, I'd have liked this film a lot more.

Monday, October 5, 2015

Opportunity Missed

The Pope came to the United States and, as chance would have it, his visit coincided with a political effort to defund Planned Parenthood (PP), the major abortion provider in the United States. A series of sting videos indicated that PP was profiting by selling the parts of the aborted fetuses. Moreover, the Pope was scheduled to address the Congress where the Speaker, John Boehner, and the Minority Leader, Nancy Pelosi, are both Catholics. The stars had aligned in the fight against abortion and the Pope pressed Congress on the issue... of climate change.

The Papacy is not necessarily political. Though the very teachings of Catholicism come down on one side or another of a great many political issues (e.g. abortion, capital punishment, gay marriage, welfare, etc.), it is not incumbent on the Pope to lobby or cajole governments to follow these teachings. Render unto Caesar what is Caesar's. But this Pope isn't that kind of Pope. He has been more political than his predecessor and has taken a decidedly leftist view of the world. Clearly, Pope Francis has embraced climate change and he takes a dim view of capitalism. So one wonders why, when the table was set for a victory against abortion, he put his political capital behind climate change.

I'm not Catholic and may be missing something. Perhaps someone who follows the doings of Popes is fully aware of the reasons behind this. It's been my understanding that the Church has a very long standing opposition to abortion while this climate change interest is very recent. Pope John Paul II spoke about it but it was not top of his docket. Pope Francis has elevated it considerably.

Wednesday, October 7, 2015

Charity must be Voluntary

I had a conversation with one of the members of the legislature the other day. I said, 'I respect the fact that you believe in small government. I do, too. I also know that you're a person of faith.

'Now, when you die and get to the meeting with St. Peter, he's probably not going to ask you much about what you did about keeping government small. But he is going to ask you what you did for the poor. You better have a good answer.'

John Kasich, Ohio Governor and Presidential Candidate

Let's ignore the separation of church and state for the moment and just ponder this future conversation with St. Peter.

St. Peter: What did you do for the poor, John?

Kasich: I arranged for tax dollars to pay for their healthcare.

St. Peter: You took monies coerced from the citizens of your state and directed them to the poor to benefit you in the afterlife?

Kasich: What? Coerced?

St. Peter: I presume the citizens were required to pay the tax or suffer some penalty of law?

Kasich: Well, yeah. But it was for charity.

St. Peter: You realize it isn't charity unless it's voluntary?

Kasich: Funding through voluntary contributions isn't the way government does things.

St. Peter: Taking money from the person who earned it and giving it to the poor is not a virtue. Good intentions do not change the fact that it was government-sanctioned theft. How much of *your* money did you give to the poor?

Imagine if, instead of having government fund this directly, Governor Kasich funneled the money to a church-run charity that did *exactly* the same thing. By his own admission, he is funding healthcare for the poor because he wants to have a good answer for St. Peter. This is about his religious convictions, not secular governance. Though it would have the same end by different means, there would be a firestorm of protest. If the Catholic Church is all in favor of the government coercing the taxpayer to fund the poor - a task that was once handled by churches, shouldn't it be automatically opposed as a mix of church and state? Hasn't government funding allowed churches to direct their money to other issues? By taking the expense of supporting the poor from churches, isn't that a contribution to churches?

Government cannot engage in charity. Everything government does is founded on its monopoly on the use of force.

Only government can 'legally' initiate force to make people comply. Non-governmental entities that initiate force are called criminals.

Saturday, October 10, 2015

Syria Strategy in Shambles

President Obama is currently back on his gun control crusade, now considering executive action that he once said was beyond his authority. Just like immigration reform was beyond his authority until he did it anyway. And Congress let him get away with it. Before the Oregon shooting, Obama had moved from the 'success' of his Iran Deal to his Climate Change Crusade. He wants to talk about anything not related to his Middle East policy. Here are a few things that have happened regarding Syria in just the last month or so:

Aug 23: Even proponents say Iran Nuke Deal just kicks the can 15 years down the road.[21]

Sept 3: Iran dismisses claims that Iran Deal will restrict their military ambitions. Even as Obama was still trying to push the deal in Congress, Iran is diminishing its value.[22]

Sept 9: Russian troops in joint operations with Syrian forces. This is not good news for the anti-Assad rebels that we are supporting.[23]

Sept 10: Democrats defeat Republican effort to nix Iran Deal.[24]

Sept 11: NATO surprised by Russian move into Syria. This speaks wonders for our intelligence agencies.[25]

Sept 12: Look, Iran has more uranium than we thought. Somehow, I suspect Obama had this information related to him in a Presidential Daily Brief some time in advance of his lobbying Congress to pass his nuke deal.[26]

Sept 14: Russia deploys tanks at Syrian airfield. The US doesn't have any tanks in Syria. We are suddenly losing the arms race in Syria.[27]

Sept 16: Ballistic Missiles development not part of deal. Well, that's good news. We've delayed nukes for 15 years - if they don't cheat (pay no attention to the story above about unexpected uranium) - but they will have fully developed delivery capacity waiting for the warheads. Awesome.[28]

Sept 18: Russia deploys Tactical Fighter Jets to Syrian base. This can't be good. First tanks, now fighters jets.[29]

Sept 22: Russia establishing bases in Syria. And now Syria is more firmly in the Russian sphere of influence. While the US draws out of the Middle East, Russia is gladly moving in.[30]

Sept 27: Russia and Iran ally with Syria's Assad, making Obama's official policy of Assad's removal all that much more unlikely.[31]

Sept 29: Iran purchase aircraft and satellites from Russia. Yes, Iran is also firmly in the Russian sphere of influence.[32]

Oct 1: Iranian troops headed to Syria to help Assad. US Syrian policy in collapse.[33]

Oct 1: Russia begins airstrikes in Syria, but not against ISIS. US supported rebels targeted.[34]

Oct 2: Putin declares Syrian no-fly zone. The US used to have a monopoly on Middle Eastern no-fly zones.[35]

Oct 4: US proposes ramping up pressure on ISIS in Syria. We're getting outmaneuvered! We'd better do something soon.[36]

Oct 7: Iran refuses any further talks with US. After a complete victory like the nuke deal, there's no point in more talks.[37]

Oct 7: Russia supports Syrian offensive with cruise missiles. The US used to have a monopoly on Middle Eastern cruise missile use.[38]

Oct 9: Iran Nuke Deal violates federal law. That's all well and good but it's not going to prevent President Obama from lifting sanctions. Federal law hasn't been an impediment to much of his policy so far.[39]

Oct 10: US abandons training Syrian resistance to combat ISIS. Yes, time to throw in the towel.[40]

Obama was never serious about fighting ISIS. He had to 'do something' because of the beheading of US citizens. He did as little as he could. If I know that, Russia and Iran know that too. And they have gladly moved in to take advantage of American weakness. As Obama shows weakness at each provocation, America's enemies get bolder. This next year is not going to be a good one for US foreign policy and that's why the gun control crusade is a top priority again.

Friday, October 16, 2015

Sanders vs. Carson?

Politico has an interesting graphic that shows how much each candidate has raised and, more interesting, what percentage was from low dollar donations (under $200); that would be voters rather than big dollar donors. Based purely on dollars generated, Hillary is the big winner:

Candidate	Millions of $
Clinton	29.9
Sanders	26.2
Carson	20.8
Bush	13.4
Cruz	12.2
Walker	7.4
Fiorina	6.8

Rubio	5.8
Kasich	4.4
Christie	4.2

Only the top 10 are listed but Clinton is the big winner with Sanders very close and Carson as the dominant Republican. Keep in mind that the Republican field is much larger and the money is spread among more candidates. Though the Democrats look to be the big money draws, the entire field only collected $58.1 million while the Republican field collected $85.3 million. But here is where it gets interesting. When considering the source of that money, it is revealing to see how much enthusiasm is coming from the voters vs. the big donors:

Candidate	% Small Donation
Sanders	77%
Trump	71%
Carson	60%
Huckabee	59%
Paul	51%
Fiorina	48%
Cruz	43%
Webb	42%
Walker	36%
Rubio	21%

Again, only the top 10 are listed but Sanders is clearly supported by the base. Only 17% of Hillary's money came from small donations. And she smashes JEB, who only saw 7% of his from small donations. These under $200 donations are from Ma & Pa

Kettle, the average voter. One more graphic to show dollars from small donors:

Candidate	Millions of $
Sanders	20.2
Carson	12.5
Cruz	5.2
Clinton	5.1
Fiorina	3.3
Trump	2.8
Walker	2.7
Paul	1.3
Rubio	1.2
Bush	0.9

Sanders has raised four times what Hillary has from the base voter while Carson has collected more than double his nearest competitor. Trump is a special case since he has not sought, and does not need, donations and has them anyway; he has utterly trounced JEB in small donations, who does have a fundraising machine.

Obviously, the election is more than a year away and the first votes aren't cast until February. However, it is clear which candidates are generating enthusiasm from the voters and which are not. If the current pattern holds (which it won't), we might be looking at Sanders vs. Carson. I can hardly wait to accuse every Democrat I meet of being a racist for opposing a black man.

Saturday, October 17, 2015

Crimson Peak

Set late in the 19th century, our movie opens with a battered Edith (Mia Wasikowska) standing in a snowy landscape announcing that she believes in ghosts. The movie then picks up when she is ten years old and her mother died, only to return as a horrifying ghost who warns her to stay away from Crimson Peak. Fourteen years later, Edith is busy writing her great American novel - dismissed as a 'ghost story' by her publisher - when Baronet Thomas Sharpe (Tom Hiddleston) arrives. Edith is enchanted by him but her father dislikes him. It is clear that Thomas and his sister Lucille (Jessica Chastain) have some plot in mind regarding Edith.

The ghosts that haunt Edith are the scariest part of the movie and also mostly irrelevant to the story. Beyond giving her a heads-up that she is in danger, they are mostly just there to offer the occasional scare. In that way, they mirror the book she has written, which she described not as a ghost story but a 'story with a ghost.' Though I generally like Tom Hiddleston - his turn as Loki in the Marvel Universe has been great fun - he just isn't charming enough to have so easily seduced Edith. Maybe if she had been portrayed as some plain Jane shut-in, I might have accepted it, but Edith is a very confident woman with strong opinions. And yet she is readily seduced when he compliments her writing. Another oddity was the apparent poverty of Sir Thomas. Later developments show that he had come into money but it has done him no good. Why not? Where did this money go?

Another interesting bit was the repeated warning from her mother. The first time, she was a child and may have dismissed it in adulthood. But then her mother returns, coincident with the arrival of Sir Thomas. And Sir Thomas has a mine that produces vibrant red clay. Hmm. Mother said to beware of Crimson Peak and this fellow arrives with a jar brilliant red clay. Maybe I should ask about Crimson Peak? It just seems that she would be more aware of the color red. Of course, such warnings are not meant to be followed or there would be no movie.

The look of the film is very stylistic. Sir Thomas' manor house is in ruins. The roof is gone so that leaves and snow gather in a patch in the main hall. It is very odd to have the characters standing on the staircase and watching snow fall within the house. It was almost like a small courtyard. Of course, we know that Edith is wealthy and must wonder why there wasn't an immediate effort to patch the roof. Well, that would ruins some of the atmosphere of the place. The ghosts aren't the typical transparent phantoms that one expects. There are two primary types of ghost. First, we see the inky black ghost that has tendrils of black smoke trailing its movements. These were the scarier ones since they were more likely to grab her. BOO! Then there were the creepy red ones, that looked to be made of red clay. These looked to be skinned and transparent versions of the people they represented.

Doctor Alan McMichael (Charlie Hunnam) is an old friend of Edith's and apparently an avid reader of Arthur Conan Doyle. It is also clear that he has feelings for Edith and is distrustful of Sir Thomas. While Edith runs into ghosts in England, Alan detects back in America. He discovers something that sends him on a rescue mission to England where, despite his suspicions, he is utterly unprepared when his suspicions prove true. This was rather annoying. It was as if he was really bright up until the script required him to be stupid. And then he was.

Not great but worth seeing. Maybe wait for it on cable.

Saturday, October 24, 2015

Tony Blair's Apology

Former Prime Minister Tony Blair has apologized for the Iraq

War, even going so far to take some responsibility for the rise of ISIS. I am truly perplexed at why he has done this. There is nothing to gain by this apology. If he thought he was hounded when he held that it was a good decision, just wait for the attacks now that he has admitted guilt for a bad decision. Sure, he has no political future to protect but history will not be kind.

There was a brief period when Tony Blair was the leader of the Free World. President Clinton was happily ignoring America's traditional leadership role that seemed so unimportant with the end of the Cold War. Blair took up the mantle and pushed for action in Kosovo, dragging Clinton along. President Bush resumed America's leadership role. President Obama has discarded it and there hasn't been a Tony Blair to pick it up. The Free World is currently rudderless and the consequences are everywhere.

Tony Blair is not responsible for ISIS, not even partially. This is post hoc ergo propter hoc logic. If Blair must blame someone, he should be pointing his finger at Barack Obama. Iraq had been won and was surprisingly stable after the US Surge in 2007. The US Military was the foundation of that stability. Had that foundation remained - as it had in places like Germany, Japan, and South Korea, ISIS could not have taken root. Obama and Biden were proclaiming Iraq as a success of *their* administration in 2010! Then we pulled out all US troops, collapse followed, and Blair is accepting some blame? It almost reminds one of Vietnam where the US achieved success in the Paris Peace Accords - Kissinger received a Nobel Peace Prize - and then, in the wake of Watergate, the Congress cut all support to South Vietnam. North Vietnam violated the peace accords and the US did nothing. Collapse and millions of boat people followed. Bush and Blair won the war but it was up to their successors to keep the peace. Blair has inexplicably accepted blame for the failures of others.

Unless he has some terminal illness that has prompted this

apology, Blair will live to regret it. He did not learn from his contemporary, Bill Clinton: deny everything. By apologizing, Blair has admitted guilt. Imagine if Bill Clinton suddenly apologized to all the women who accused him of misconduct, if he apologized for not killing Bin Laden when he had the chance, for suborning perjury, or for lying to the American people about 'not having sex with that woman.' Would he rise in esteem for having confessed his faults or fall for admitting guilt? Imagine the campaign ads against his wife that would be nothing but Bill admitting guilt contrasted with Hillary blaming a 'vast rightwing conspiracy.' Yes, it would be catastrophic. But Clinton is too good a politician to ever do something so stupid; such is not the case for Blair.

Of course, Blair's apology will be used to bludgeon George W. Bush, the prime mover and shaker of the Iraq War. Perhaps he expects to get the Colin Powell treatment. Maybe from the US press but probably not from the British press.

Tuesday, October 27, 2015

Monkeys to Mars

Monkeys are heading to MARS: Russian scientists are training macaques to solve puzzles so they can travel to space in 2017 (but is it a one-way trip?)

- *Russian scientists are preparing four monkeys for space travel to Mars*
- *The animals are being trained three hours a day to use a joystick*
- *Each of the macaques will then be taught to solve maths tasks and puzzles*
- *Experts hope to send the fully-trained monkeys to Mars by 2017*
- *Unclear if the mission will be one way or if the animals will return*

Monkeys paved the way for us to reach the moon and now Russian scientists are hoping the animals will be key to getting a human colony to Mars.[41]

The Russians are training an elite team of rhesus monkeys to travel to the red planet and land sometime in 2017. And so began the Planet of the Monkeys!

I think it is laughable that it is 'unclear' if the monkeys will return. Duh! Of course the monkeys won't be returning. The Russians weren't too concerned about Laika, the first dog in space. Heck, the Russians lost several cosmonauts during the Space Race thanks to their comparatively lax safety standards. Best case scenario is that one or two of the monkeys remain on an orbiter while the others land on Mars. The ones who land are there to stay. Those on the orbiter might make a return trip to determine the requirements of such a trip. The logistics of keeping the monkeys alive and well for a trip to and from Mars seem daunting. Will they be trained not to throw poop on the control panel?

We've landed probes and rovers on Mars and have had orbiters map Mars. The next logical step is getting living creatures there. The Russians have no experience beyond Low Earth Orbit (LEO), so this is more necessary for them than for the US. Still, the Russians are planning a big space program while NASA can't even get its astronauts to the International Space Station (ISS) without hitching a ride on a Russian Soyuz.

I went to the Houston Space Center several years ago and saw amazing things and heard about impressive plans. That was five years ago. Five years after Kennedy called for America to put a man on the moon, we had completed Project Mercury and were wrapping up Gemini. Today, we don't even have a vessel for our astronauts to fly. The closest thing is the SpaceX Dragon which is currently delivering supplies to the ISS. Yes, we can't get monkeys in space but the Russians are going to send some to Mars. Who won the Space Race? Who won the Cold War?

Sunday, November 1, 2015

The Martian

The movie opens with 6 astronauts already on Mars, busy doing their various research. Mark Whatney (Matt Damon) is happily noting the consistency of the dirt. He is the mission botanist. It is then that a sandstorm is spotted with sufficient severity that the mission needs to be aborted. During the evacuation, Whatney is struck by debris and thrown into the darkness. With all signs indicating he is dead and the storm threatening to topple their only means back to space, the other astronauts lift off. When Whatney awakens to an alarm on his suit, he soon discovers his dire situation. He has no way to communicate with Earth and his food supply is limited. It will be four years before another manned mission arrives and he has less than a year of food. And so begins the problem solving.

The movie is like *Apollo 13* on steroids. Houston, we have lots of problems! But, step by step, inch by inch, Whatney overcomes his problems. And new ones arise. With the notable exception of the storm that starts the ball rolling, the science is great. It really did have that Apollo 13 feel as Whatney and NASA worked through every problem, figuring how to put a square peg in a round hole. The geek references were always fun; the Council of Elrond was played quite nicely, especially since Boromir (Sean Bean) was in attendance.

Though the cast is extensive, the movie is entirely focused on Whatney. Where Ed Harris shared dominance with Tom Hanks in *Apollo 13*, in this movie, everyone else was secondary. Looking at the billing, it is surprising that Kristen Wiig was listed third when she had such a minor role. Here is a movie about making tough decisions or solving difficult problems; her character did neither.

It is a long movie but never boring. Thumbs up.

Monday, November 2, 2015

Distrust the Candidate

Immigration is one of the biggest issues of this election season and most of the Republicans are on the wrong side of the debate. Jeb Bush and Hillary Clinton have essentially the same view on immigration despite being from rival parties. Marco Rubio, who is in the process of unseating Jeb as the establishment's preferred candidate, tried to get amnesty passed several years ago but has since disavowed it. Sort of. He has declared that he would not reverse Obama's Dreamer Act; that would be the one that Congress declined to pass into law but the president enforced it anyway. Hey, faithfully execute the laws is so passé. Basically, Rubio has shown his cards. He is going to claim to be a border hawk and against illegal immigration until - should he win - he is inaugurated. Then, hello amnesty! Too many Republicans have a short-sighted view on immigration.

The fastest growing immigrant group is Muslims. Islam is entirely incompatible with the First Amendment. Rather than forcing new immigrants to live under the rules that they knew existed when they *chose* to immigrate here, we are seeing self-censorship of anything that might upset Muslims. Those who don't practice self-censorship are the bad guys in most media reporting. "If you hadn't drawn that cartoon of Muhammad, you wouldn't have been shot. It's your own damn fault!" There will come a time when an area is majority Muslim and it will vote for Sharia law. This is a when, not an if. Muslim immigration has done wonders for Paris and Stockholm but I'm sure it will work out much better for us.

Rubio probably thinks that because he is Hispanic, he will benefit from an Amnesty. He is delusional. Amnesty is Republican suicide. Ever notice how the Democrats are so concerned that Republicans will never win the White House again if they don't change their views on illegal immigration? If the other party were ruining its chanced to compete with mine, I certainly wouldn't mind and absolutely wouldn't give them advise that might *harm* my party's chances. Sure, the Democrats only want what's best for Republicans. BS! Republicans, being stupid, have swallowed this nonsense and are prepared to give millions of votes to the Democrats by passing some form of amnesty.

Amnesty is an existential threat to the party and yet most of the candidates are in favor. Few have learned from history. Republicans lost California thanks to the last amnesty. Lose one more big state and their presidential prospects will vanish for many years thereafter.

This is why Trump still dominates. Carson and Cruz are on the same page with him but Trump is the one who trail blazed the issue and he may ride it all the way to the Presidency.

Tuesday, November 3, 2015

Why the Terrorists are Winning

Atheist: 'Okay For Those on The Left to Critique, Mock, Deride Christianity, But Islam Gets a Free Pass'

An atheist professor said Tuesday that it's acceptable to criticize Christians but not Muslims, because he does not "fear" retaliation from Christians.

"I know what keeps me from critiquing Islam on my blog is just fear," Phil Zuckerman said at a discussion on religious liberty at Georgetown University in Washington, D.C. "I've got three kids.

"So I know I can say anything about Christianity or Mormonism, and I'm not living in fear, which is a testament to Christianity and Mormonism, and that's wonderful. Thank you," said Zuckerman, who is a self-described atheist and professor of secular studies at Pitzer College in Claremont, Calif.[42]

With previous enemies, the United States has been only too

happy to demean and dehumanize them. Watch some of the Disney cartoons that were anti-axis. The Japanese were depicted in a way that is now considered extremely racist. There was no fear of upsetting Hitler, Mussolini, or Emperor Hirohito. They were the enemy. In war, it is often necessary to dehumanize the enemy lest the horror of what is being done cripple the war effort. There is a reason that Muslims say that Jews are descended from pigs and America is the Great Satan.

I am not proposing that we start some propaganda campaign that vilifies all Muslims but we sure as heck should not be afraid to merely point out some obvious issues. As the article notes, Muslim bakeries also refused to make a cake for a gay wedding but there was no firestorm of protest. Why not? Fear. You want to see a real War on Women? Go to a Muslim country and take a look at the Burqas and that women can't leave the house unescorted by a male relative. Driving a car? Certainly not in Saudi Arabia. Gay rights? Ha! ISIS tosses gay people from tall buildings to their death. Iran publicly hangs gay people from cranes. But George W. Bush kept telling us that Islam is a religion of peace.

Arabic is the fastest growing language group in the United States. Tens of thousands of Syrians are coming to America thanks to Obama's brilliant Middle East strategy. This only serves to give the professor growing cause to be fearful. Several of the crazed gunmen in recent years were legal Muslim immigrants. The Boston Marathon Bombers were Muslim immigrants who were on welfare! We were supporting them with tax dollars while they were planning to kills us! The Chattanooga shooter was a legal Muslim immigrant. More than a dozen others have been arrested before they were able to carry out plots against America. This after we created a Department of Homeland Security.

In cases like these, deport the rest of the family. If this is the sort of fruit that these immigrants are bearing, that family tree needs to be uprooted and sent packing. Of course, that won't happen until the problem gets much, much worse.

The US has not seen the sort of assassinations of critics of Islam that have occurred in Europe, Africa, and Asia. Professor Zuckerman is overly cautious. However, it is only a matter of time before it arrives on our shores, all the more likely thanks to our suicidal immigration laws. In the long game, Islam is stealing a march (as Wellington said of Napoleon). Why kill us now if they can demographically overwhelm us in several decades? Europe is well on the way to being Eurostan.

Saturday, November 7, 2015

Jindal's Misconception

Governor Jindal of Louisiana has challenged Senator Cruz of Texas to a debate on Obamacare. Politically, this is a shrewd move. Cruz (10.5%) polls much higher than Jindal (0.7%) and Cruz has also declared that he is willing to do as many debates as possible. However, his choice of debate topics is risky.

"You get Ted Cruz who wants to shut down the government, but he's never even come up with his own plan," Jindal said. "We've written our own plan and campaigned on it, rather than just complaining about Obamacare."

I have not read Jindal's alternative to Obamacare but, whatever it may be, it will remain an overstep of Constitutional authority. The federal government has no place in healthcare. There is no amendment, no clause, no delegated power on the subject. As such, the Tenth Amendment returns it to the states or the people; the federal government should be silent on the issue. States are another matter. If Bobby Jindal wanted to develop a healthcare law for Louisiana, that's fine by me. Oregon and Massachusetts both had healthcare laws prior to Obamacare. Medicare and Medicaid remain intact. This is likely the argument that Cruz will offer. Replacing one unconstitutional law with another - even if it is better and less mandatory - would still be wrong. Healthcare should return to the states, counties, cities, or even individuals to decide. How is Jindal going to reply to that?

Trust in government is at a low ebb and proposing a new government program, even to replace an unpopular one, is the wrong path to take this election season. The voters don't want the NSA to listen to them a little less, they want the NSA to not listen at all. If you simply repeal Obamacare, all returns to what it was beforehand, which was much less expensive than now. The pendulum is swinging back from big intrusive government toward smaller, hands-off government, most especially among Republican primary voters.

I like Bobby Jindal, but I don't think this will improve his standing. Unless some of the higher tier candidates crash and burn, Jindal isn't going anywhere this time around.

Keystone XL Pipeline

After a 7 year review and only days after Canada requested that the approval process be placed on hold, President Obama rejected the XL pipeline for environmental reasons. Of course, the best thing for the environment would have been to approve the pipeline. How could that be?

First, the Canadian oil sands are going to be drilled and burned regardless of our decision. Therefore, if it is going to be exploited, we should be looking to make it as clean as possible. With the US rejecting it, Canada will instead have to build a pipeline to British Columbia and ship it to China. China does not have a record of environmental friendliness; there is a reason so many Chinese are wearing dust masks in the smog-clogged cities. As the US is shutting coal plants, China is building them at a rapid clip. Gallon for gallon, the oil would produce a lot less pollution if the US refined and burned it than any other option. Again, if it is going to be exploited, our best option from an environmentalist viewpoint is to route it to the cleanest option.

Second, as the oil sands are going to be used, someone is going to build a pipeline and profit from it. Either it is going to British Columbia or to Houston. If it goes to BC, the US gets little if any economic benefit from it. On the other hand, if it goes to Houston, the United States will build the pipeline and get value-added benefit for transporting and processing it. Refusing the project does not stop it, it only means the US economy will not benefit from it.

Third, there are already half a million miles of oil and natural gas pipelines crisscrossing the United States. Another two thousand miles is a miniscule increase in the overall network. Moreover, the safety record of pipelines is much better than the alternative means of transport: trains or trucks. Over the years, I've seen lots of stories about hazardous spills from overturned trucks and derailed trains but I can't recall any related to broken pipelines.

It took 7 years to come to the wrong factual decision. However, it does satisfy the greens who are a major part of the Democrat base. This was a political decision, not a practical or rational one.

Bernie Sanders: Incompetent Campaigner

After the Democrat debate, Jim Webb and Lincoln Chaffey dropped out of the race, which left only Hillary Clinton, Bernie Sanders, and Martin O'Malley. Thanks to Bernie announcing that he didn't care about Hillary's "damned emails," he took character off the table as a reason to choose between them. If character is not an issue, then it comes down to policies. Hillary and Bernie voted the same almost 80% of the time while they were in the Senate together. Policy-wise, they are pretty close. Since the debate, Hillary has made up lost ground. In October, she was polling at 46% but has risen 10 points. Sanders has also risen but only by 4 points to 31%. O'Malley finally registers in the polls at a paltry 2%. This according to the FOX News poll.

If Sanders is serious about winning the nomination (I don't think he is), he has to make the case that he is a better candidate. With his views relatively close to Hillary's stated views, he needs to tack toward something that differentiates them. Those 'damned emails' are a real scandal that has deserved far more attention than they have gotten. However, if a Republican mentions them, it is instantly viewed as partisan and therefore discarded by Democrat voters. Bernie could make a bipartisan case and deliver a serious hit on her ethics and honesty. Sanders is essentially an isolationist as far as foreign policy, so he could make hay with Hillary's Libyan adventure.

"We Came, We Saw, He died."
Hillary Clinton on Muammar Gaddafi

She was proud of the intervention then, but in the aftermath of Benghazi, this is a monumental failure waiting for an opponent to exploit. It is almost certainly going to come up in the Presidential Debates if Hillary is the nominee. Sanders may as well use it, if only to prepare her for the inevitable attacks later. After all, it was Al Gore who first used Willie Horton against Dukakis. How about the Russian Reset; are things going swimmingly between us and Putin thanks to her smart diplomacy? Maybe she can dump that disaster on Kerry. Hillary was proud of the amount of miles she traveled during her tenure as Secretary of State; what is her legacy? Treaties? Ally-building?

Maybe her time as Secretary of State was unimpressive but she still has her time in the Senate. She voted in favor of invading both Afghanistan and Iraq. Of course, like many Democrats, she recanted on Iraq and voted against the 2007 Iraq surge. Her most famous quote as Senator is probably this:

I am sick and tired of people who say that if you debate and you disagree with this administration, somehow you're not patriotic, and we should stand up and say, "WE ARE AMERICANS AND WE HAVE A RIGHT TO DEBATE AND DISAGREE WITH ANY ADMINISTRATION!"

I completely agree though I don't think she does. Disagreement with Obama has too often been labeled as racism and disagreement with her is sexist. In any case, the accomplishments in the Senate are not impressive. I know of no legislation with her name on it (I count that as an achievement since I would rather *not* have new laws but her base disagrees with me) and her voting record is unremarkable. Those votes for Afghanistan and Iraq are a big problem for the base but Bernie is letting them slide.

Hillary is a weak candidate. She is such a weak candidate that a little-known senator in his first term was able to defeat her for the nomination in 2008. In much the way Sanders is treating her now, she did not attack Obama despite some easy and obvious issues. McCain opted to follow Hillary's losing strategy and, unsurprisingly, lost. Now, Sanders is no Barack Obama but if he made an issue of Hillary's lack of achievement, her perceived untrustworthiness, and her scandals, he could eek out the nomination. I don't think he'll do that; in which case I suspect he has already resigned himself to losing. However, even in loss he can win influence. Hillary parleyed her loss into Secretary of State.

I've seen a meme on Facebook that congratulated Sanders for dismissing the 'damned emails,' calling him a gentleman for it. Sad to say, but gentlemen lose elections. Bob Dole was a gentleman. John McCain was a gentleman. Mitt Romney was a gentleman. Romney was savaged by the Obama campaign, made responsible for the death of a former employee's wife, painted as a bully for an incident from high school, falsely accused of not paying his taxes, and on and on. Yes, it would be nice if elections had some sort of Marquis of Queensbury rules but they don't. If you can't reply in kind, you're probably going to lose. Of course, since Sanders is playing the gentleman and also losing, Hillary is content to have a 'civil' primary campaign. But if the situation were reversed, Hillary would not let an email scandal or the like be ignored.

Sunday, November 8, 2015

What a Difference Party-Affiliation Makes

It appears that the media is going through Ben Carson's biography *Gifted Hands* (1990) with a fine toothcomb in order to demonstrate that he is not qualified for the Presidency. So far, there have been stories about his informal invitation to attend West Point, his self-reported but unconfirmable (by the media) violent youth, his meeting of General Westmoreland, and even his claim that he ushered some white students into a lab to protect them from a riot in the wake of Martin Luther King Jr.'s assassination. All of these take place in the mid to late 60s. I suspect more such attacks will commence when the reporters read the chapters that cover the 70s and 80s. This is fine. Past writings are fair game and a politician should be made to clarify or defend such writings.

Of course, Ben Carson is not the first black man to run for president who had a biography in his past. Indeed, Barack Obama had two biographies: *Dreams from My Father* (1995) and *The Audacity of Hope* (2006). Between these two books, Obama admits drunk driving, regular use of marijuana in his teens, use of cocaine, a communist mentor, a political kickoff at the home of a former terrorist, and admiration for a reverend who 'damned' America in a sermon. Oddly, the media was mostly disinterested in these biographies and the revelations therein. Yes, he had to answer for Reverend Wright in a speech where he placed Wright's comments in historical context. After that, the matter was dropped by the media. Interestingly, Hillary Clinton grabbed hold of it in a later debate and said that Wright's anti-American sermon immediately in the wake of 9/11 was intolerable. Further, she pointed out that we don't choose our family, but we do chose our church. John McCain gave Obama a pass on Reverend Wright and went on to lose the election.

A Democratic candidate admitted crimes and associations with communists and terrorists and the media shrugged. Nothing to see here. A Republican candidate - at worst - boasts of events in his youth and is branded a liar! No double-standard at all.

Friday, November 13, 2015

The Rising Tide of Terrorism

"We have contained them."
- President Barack Obama regarding ISIS, Good Morning America this morning

A few hours later, Paris erupted in violence with Muslim men screaming Allah Akbar as they gunned down and blew up more than a hundred French citizens in various locations in the city. It is not yet known if the attacker were faux refugees from Syria. In February, ISIS did declare plans to infiltrate Europe with terrorists. Mission accomplished? How many hundreds of thousands of refugees have already arrived in Europe and what portion are terrorists. Germany has seen many new refugees vanish from venues provided to house them. Might some of those have made their way across the mostly borderless Eurozone to join the attack?

I don't keep up with French politics and therefore don't know what has been done in the wake of Charlie Hebdo attacks in January of this year. I would say that the evidence shows that not enough was done. At the moment, a curfew has been imposed and the borders have been closed. But the problem is already inside the borders. France has a Muslim population of 6% as of 2007. Where might that stand now? What percentage of those 4 million Muslims are likely to be 'radicalized?' Even at the low number of 1% of them, that is 40,000 Jihadists already within the borders. Sadly, the number is higher than 1%. That's a big problem.

Elsewhere in Europe, England is 5% Muslim, Spain is 3.7% Muslim, Italy 2.6%, Sweden 5.1%, and - prior to the big push - Germany was 1.9%. This is not to accuse all Muslims of being terrorists but the terrorist come from this population. The Lutherans, the Roman Catholics, and the Anglicans aren't causing the problem.

With this in mind, the US is almost 1% Muslim and this is the fastest growing migrant population. We have already seen radicalization in the population and yet the president is pushing to have 10,000 Syrian refugees resettled in the US. The Tsarnaev brothers (Boston Marathon bombers) came to the US as refugees.

Like it or not, there is a religious war in progress and one side doesn't realize it. The aggressors use religious words and phrases: Infidel, Allah Akbar, Great Satan. The timing could hardly be worse with the West suffering a civilization breakdown with the rise of multiculturalism (no culture is better than another), political correctness (self-censorship), and victim culture (large subsets of the population are now victims who have a 'right' to not be offended). Heck, Jihadists have been adopted into the victim culture, an oppressed group that we must understand, not destroy.

Sadly, like we have done as 9/11 has faded further into history, France will likely get into the fray briefly and then lapse back into apathy. I especially don't expect President Hollande to become the next de Gaulle. These attacks will certainly benefit the more nativist parties throughout Europe. Look for Hungary's example to spread.

Saturday, November 14, 2015

A Tale of Two Stories

French TV BLASTS Racist Republicans for Blaming Attacks on

Refugees[43]
-    U.S. Uncut, Nov 14, 2015

At least one man linked to Paris attacks registered as refugee[44]
-    Yahoo! News, Nov 14, 2015

I did enjoy how the first story claims to have the correct response to Islamophobia. Of course, I don't think there is any such thing as Islamophobia. Let's look at the definition of a phobia:

A phobia is a type of anxiety disorder, usually defined as a persistent fear of an object or situation in which the sufferer commits to great lengths in avoiding, typically disproportional to the actual danger posed, often being recognized as irrational.

There is nothing irrational about fearing Islam, even for a Muslim. Sunnis and Shi'ites have been slaughtering one another for centuries. ISIS is actively seeking to infiltrate other countries to commit exactly the sort of atrocities that just occurred in Paris. Certainly, the governments of the West have not gone to disproportionate lengths to avoid Islam. No, they view Muslims as victims who need special treatment and understanding. It is obvious that the West has failed to take adequate precautions against Islam. There is no phobia when the fear is entirely justified. Of course, the term was created to allow Islam access to victimhood and the right to not be offended. Ah, multiculturalism and political correctness, is there no end to your bounty?

Though Europe is up in arms now, I fully expect this to die down and things to drift back to the status quo. After all, the US absorbed a 9/11 attack and quit fighting without winning. Europe will do the same. It will have to get much, much worse before the West commits to victory.

Sunday, November 15, 2015

Crashing the Party

During the tenure of George W. Bush as President, the

Republican party suffered down the ticket. Nine Senate seats (and control of the Senate in 2006), 42 House seats (plus control of the House in 2006), 7 governorships, and 324 seats in the various legislatures & assemblies through the states. which saw the switch of control in 13 chambers. When the Democrats took the Presidency in 2008, James Carville looked at this recent history and viewed it as a generational switch to the Democrats, a new period like that from 1932 to 1952 of Democrat control of the Presidency.

During the tenure of Barack Obama as President, the Democrats have suffered down the ticket. 13 Senate seats (and control), 69 House seats (and control), 11 governorships, and 913 legislators at the state level, shifting control in 30 chambers. President Obama has been a disaster for his party's elective offices. Will anyone, other than me or someone on FOX News, ask Carville about his prediction?

This clearly demonstrates that Obama is not as popular as he is portrayed in the media. Following his prescriptions for the nation, his party had suffered massive setbacks, far worse than the supposedly hated Bush inflicted upon his party. If the Republicans manage to retake the Presidency and the new president is just as unpopular as Bush was, the Democrats will still be in the hole from where they stood in 2008, especially at the state level. This shift in power at the state level does not bode well for the 2020 gerrymandering that will greatly impact the Congress from 2020 to 2030.

Looking at this, it makes one wonder why the Republicans in Congress are so cowed by the President. With all this growing strength, why the continued spinelessness?

Tuesday, November 17, 2015

The Nuance of JEB

Yet again, Jeb has taken a stand at odds with the people who must vote for him if he is to win the Republican nomination.

While Republican, and even Democrat, governors are lining up in the wake of the Paris attacks to refuse to accept Syrian refugees and Speaker Ryan is suggesting a pause in such refugees, Jeb announces that he would not stop accepting refugees. No, he says he would deal with the problem in Syria. Gee, that's great Jeb but, with Obama as president, that isn't going to happen. Deal with what is, not what you wish it were. Again and again, Jeb appears to be completely oblivious to the current political realities. He calls illegal immigration an 'act of love' and looks ready to try to push his brother's failed 2007 Amnesty. The voters keep announcing what they want and Trump espouses it. Voila! Trump is in the lead. Jeb then bashes Trump and his poll numbers sink further. Despite repeated restarts of his campaign, he remains tone deaf to his electorate.

Jeb is ever eager to announce his prior gubernatorial experience in a year when candidates with no political experience at all are leading by double digits. The voters have seen the wonders worked by 'experienced' politicians with decades in government and the results speak for themselves. Trump and Carson, two men with zero elective experience lead the field. In such an environment, running on elective experience is counter-productive but Jeb still hasn't figured that out.

It is time for Jeb to join fellow governors Bobby Jindal and Scott Walker and bow out. Jeb is in the mold of Romney, Dole, and McCain. They were all moderate Republicans with plenty of experience and no desire to attack the Democrat nominee. Jeb has more venom for Trump in the primary than he will ever have for Hillary in the general election. That is a losing strategy. Even his brother would likely have lost in 2004 if not for the Swift Boat Veterans attacking Kerry. Given a choice between the perfect candidate who will lose and an imperfect one who will win, choose the winner.

Wednesday, November 18, 2015

Illegal Immigrants can also be Terrorists

Apparently, some of those refugees that President Obama wants to admit to the country over the objection of half the governors are impatient. Yes, they decided to cross the border independent of the president's demands for Syrian asylum.

EXCLUSIVE — CONFIRMED: 8 Syrians Caught at Texas Border in Laredo

Two federal agents operating under the umbrella of U.S. Customs and Border Protection (CBP) are claiming that eight Syrian illegal aliens attempted to enter Texas from Mexico in the Laredo Sector.[45]

Keep in mind that these are the ones we caught. Recall that 10 to 20 million - perhaps more - illegal immigrants have already sneaked into the country. These are the people that George W. Bush, Barack Obama, JEB, Hillary Clinton, Marco Rubio, et al. can hardly wait to legalize via amnesty. Let's do a bit of calculation here. Back in 1986, three million were granted amnesty, so this current crop of 10 to 20 million (or more) have crossed the borders since then. Say 30 years, just for a nice round number. Also, let's stick to the 10 to 20 million range. That means anywhere from 330 thousand to 670 thousand foreigners manage to sneak across our borders EVERY year since 1986. On the low side, that is about a thousand a day who are successful! And we just caught 8 Syrians. How many did we NOT catch? I'm sure it's nothing to worry about.

Thursday, November 19, 2015

Ouroboros

An ouroboros is a snake that eats its own tail. Such creatures have existed in many mythologies though the most noted is probably Jormungandr, the Norse serpent that encircles the world. It is fated to slay Thor during Ragnarök (Norse Doomsday) while also being killed by the thunder god. I mention this because the Democratic Party is starting to resemble an ouroboros. A few months ago, I noted here that most Democratic Presidents would be found lacking as far as racial sensitivity was concerned. At that time, the problem was Thomas Jefferson and Andrew Jackson. Now the issue is Woodrow Wilson.

Princeton Students Take Over President's Office, Demand Erasure Of Woodrow Wilson

Black Lives Matter activists at Princeton University have taken over the president's office and say they won't leave until the school acknowledges former U.S. president Woodrow Wilson as a racist and renames all buildings currently honoring him on campus.[46]

As more and more Democratic Presidents are attacked by Democratic constituencies, the foundation will erode. Recall, it was the Democratic Party that defended segregation and Jim Crow into the 1960s. It was Orval Faubus - Democrat Governor of Arkansas - who opposed racial integration and Dwight Eisenhower - Republican President - who federalized the national guard to enforce Brown vs. Board of Education. Eisenhower also signed the Civil Rights Acts of 1957 and 1960. Today, the only one anyone remembers is the Civil Rights Act of 1964. It should be noted that Strom Thurmond - then a Democrat - filibustered the 1957 Civil Rights act for more than 24 hours, setting a record for a one man filibuster. What about the infamous Bull Connor? Yeah, he was a Democrat. Governor George "segregation now, segregation tomorrow, segregation forever" Wallace was a Democrat.

The Ku Klux Klan was an ally of the Democratic Party from its founding, achieving its highest membership in the mid-1920s. Let's look at Klansmen who entered politics:

Harry Truman, Democrat President: Briefly dabbled with the Klan in the mid-20s, when it was at its peak. If he did join (it is in doubt), it was in order to get votes for his reelection campaign of 1924.

Robert Byrd, Democrat Senator: Achieved title of Kleagle and Exalted Cyclops but left organization in 1940s.

Hugo Black, Democrat Supreme Court Justice: Joined in early 1920s to gain votes.
Theodore Bilbo, Democrat Senator: Stated in interview that once a Klansman, always a Klansman. One had to take an oath to that effect.

Bibb Graves, Democrat Governor: Joined to improve electoral chances.

Clifford Walker, Democrat Governor: Revealed as Klansman in 1924.

George Gordon, Democrat Congressman: First Grand Dragon of Tennessee.

Benjamin Stapleton, Democrat mayor of Denver: Appointed Klan members to most positions in municipal government.

David Duke, Democrat (pre-1989) & Republican (post-1989) Legislator: Democrats' favorite Klansman because he has an R after his name these days. According to Duke, he left the KKK in 1980, which puts him in the Democrat column.

Truman is going to have to go. Half the government buildings in West Virginia are named for Robert Byrd; need to rename them all. Democrats prior to the 1960s are almost certainly going to be unacceptable to the Black Lives Matter crowd. The ones after 1960s should also be unacceptable but thanks to the deft political skills of LBJ and a compliant media, everyone now thinks that it was the Republicans - party of Lincoln, the party founded to oppose slavery - who were the slave owners and segregationists.

The Democrats have championed Political Correctness and been only too happy to attack minor incidents in their opponents' past as a reason such people should be reviled. They never expected this to be used against them, especially by those they had inculcated with PC. Oh, the irony. The poetic justice. I am curious to see how much more this ouroboros is able to devour itself.

Wednesday, November 25, 2015

Turkey Shoot

The Turks have shot down a Russian fighter jet and NATO asks why didn't Turkey just escort the jet out of Turkish airspace. The evidence in the aftermath is that Russia only just clipped a strip of land that projects - like a peninsula - into Syria. The incursion was only a few seconds. Really, Turkey, why so trigger happy?

It seems that Russian jets have been making a habit of drifting into Turkish airspace. Here's a story from October 6th:

Turkey 'cannot endure' Russian violation of airspace, president says

A war of words has broken out between Russia and NATO over Moscow's military intervention in Syria and its violation of Turkish airspace.

The row threatens to further escalate tensions over Moscow's airstrikes to support the regime of Syria's president, Bashar al-Assad. The Turkish president, Recep Tayyip Erdogan, said his country could not endure Russian violations of its airspace in its campaign in Syria and said Russia risked "losing" Turkey.[47]

Moreover, it should be remembered that Turkey and Russia have a long and troubled history. They have been at war with one another 12 times in the past 450 years. Much of the Balkans were lost during wars with the Russians. Though it has been nearly a century since they last clashed in war during World War I, they remained belligerent toward one another. Turkey became part of NATO during the Cold War, continuing the adversarial relationship. Russia is just as aware of this history and should have known that repeated poking would provoke a response.

Though no fan of Erdogan, I'm generally on Turkey's side here. Whether or not there were warnings this time around, there had been warnings in the recent past. This was not some passenger plane that was a little off course, this was an armed fighter. Russian pilots dismissed them and have paid the price. I am willing to bet that there will be an end to the airspace incursions.

That aside, this is the first time in over half a century that a Russian plane was shot down by a NATO member. Precisely this was feared when Russia joined the Syrian Civil War. Russia and NATO allies have different objectives in Syria and it is inevitable that there will be clashes. It is unlikely this will be the only one.

Theodore Roosevelt said that one should speak softly and carry a big stick. He was accused of being a jingoistic warmonger. However, there were no wars during his presidency. In fact, he won the Nobel Peace Prize for negotiating a peace between Russia and Japan during the Russo-Japanese War (1905). He sent the Great White Fleet - consisting of 16 battleships and various escorts - around the world to display American naval power. With such an outward show of strength, the warmonger never had a war. That was by design.

By contrast, Barack Obama has shown nothing but weakness and withdrawal. He talks of smart diplomacy and the right side of history but the conflicts multiply and our enemies grow stronger. For the last 7 years, we have negotiated with adversaries (Iran, Russia) and undercut our allies (Poland, Israel). The incident on the Turkish border is a direct result of the catastrophic foreign policy of the Obama Administration. Former Secretary of State Hillary Clinton shares in this disaster and promises to stay the course.

Spectre

Bond is back and so is Ernst Stavro Blofeld. After a decades long absence, Blofeld is back as the head of Spectre though his backstory has dramatically changed. The movie opens with Bond in Mexico City for Dia de los Muertos (Day of the Dead). He's on a mission to kill a man. The action that follows is ridiculous to the extreme and a return to the silliness that we saw in *Quantum of Solace*. Also echoing *Quantum of Solace*, Blofeld's secret hideout is amazingly combustible. Why do James Bond's villains use dynamite, hydrogen, and gasoline as construction materials?

Mr. Hinx (Dave Bautista) is an excellent henchmen along the lines of Odd Job and Jaws. He is pure aggression and his dialogue is next to nil. Where Jaws had steel teeth, Hinx has sharpened steel thumbnails, the better to gouge eyeballs. Unlike Odd Job and Jaws, Hinx is not some grim humorless thug. No, he spends a lot of time smiling, especially after killing someone or shooting holes in your plane. He is also surprisingly well-dressed. I hope to see him again in the next film.

Blofeld has proved a more durable villain in the movies - 8 so far - than in the novels - only appeared in 3. In the novels, Spectre and Blofeld were introduced in *Thunderball* (9th novel). Bond killed Blofeld in *You Only Live Twice* (12th novel). The movies opted to replace the Soviets with Spectre right from the start so that Blofeld and his fluffy white cat appear in almost every Sean Connery Bond film. I did like how Blofeld (Christoph Waltz) is made the architect of the previous 3 movies. The mysterious Quantum group was just a facet of Spectre and the chief villains in each of those films was just a minion of Blofeld. Blofeld is mostly unemotional and unmoved by whatever is happening. He is never angry and rarely shows anything beyond mild amusement. He plays a good host but it is just an act. Reminded me a bit of Jake Gyllenhaal in *Nightcrawler*.

The Daniel Craig period as Bond has seen a lot of more depth to the character and very few of the post-kill witticisms. In *Casino Royale*, we saw his first love - Vesper Lynd - and her death. *Quantum of Solace* was basically a waste though it does fold into the storyline of *Spectre*. In *Skyfall*, we see his childhood home and learn how he was an orphan. Here in *Spectre*, we learn of Hans Obenhauser, a man who adopted him after his parents' death. This was only ever mentioned in the short story *Octopussy* in the novels but is greatly expanded here. Wow, I really didn't see that coming.

Another interesting development is that this Bond is part of a team. M (Ralph Fiennes), Moneypenny (Namoie Harris), Q (Ben Whishaw), and Bill Tanner (Roy Kinnear) have sizeable roles that span the movie, not just the opening office bit when 007 is dispatched on his mission. Part of this has to do with how the modern world works. As Bond can't be an awesome computer hacker - very important in modern intelligence - that facet goes to Q. Also, the proliferation of cellphones means that the office is always available, thus contact to M or Moneypenny is as easy as pie. This is a departure from the novels but I welcome it.

A rarity for Bond movies, none of the Bond girls died. Daniel Craig has not shown himself to be the lady's man of previous Bonds. Though he has a beauty with him at the start, he leaves her in the room before anything happens and never returns. His only love interest here is Madeleine Swann (Lea Seydoux), who appears not to be just another ship passing in the night.

All in all, a fun Bond flick with more weight to it than others in the franchise. The series has moved into an overarching storyline, fitting it more to the mold of the Bourne movies or Harry Potter.

Friday, November 27, 2015

Mayor Asterisk

13 months after Laquan McDonald was killed by Officer Jason Van Dyke in Chicago, the dashcam video of the incident has finally been released. The 17 year-old was walking down the street with a knife in hand and refusing officers' orders. Then Van Dyke arrived. In the video, he draws his gun and suddenly

Laquan is down. Just looking at the video, I didn't understand the issue. You run around with a knife and refuse to drop it when ordered by police, you should expect to get shot. No, what bothered me is how he was just left to bleed. It wasn't until I read the story that I learned that Van Dyke had emptied his 16 round clip! Laquan was riddled with 14 bullets, the vast majority of them after he was already lying on the street. Van Dyke has been charged with first-degree murder for the incident.

As it happens, Mayor Rahm Emanuel - former Chief of Staff for President Obama - was coincidentally running for reelection as mayor. Had the dashcam video been released prior to the February election or the April run-off election, Emanuel would have had a much more difficult path to reelection. Where he had black pastors working to get him the black vote, he might instead have seen Black Lives Matter protestors at his every campaign event.

The big problem here is the mishandling from the beginning. If the video had been revealed to the public immediately and the murder charge had been levied in November of 2014, it could have been a political asset, a demonstration that the mayor was intolerant of police malfeasance. Instead, the year long delay makes one wonder what else the mayor is keeping under wraps. However, there is also the possibility that, even correctly handled, there might have been massive demonstrations that would have hurt Emanuel. I suspect that is what he feared and why it took so long to come to light.

Sunday, November 29, 2015

Victor Frankenstein

The story opens in the circus, where a young nameless hunchback (Daniel Radcliffe) is a clown and - quite surprisingly - physician. Yes, this hunchback has such a gift for anatomy that the circus allows him to treat injuries. When a trapeze artist falls and is at threat of dying, the hunchback quickly diagnoses the problem and determines a fix that saves a life. Victor Frankenstein, who is there to witness, is truly impressed. He steals the hunchback away from the circus and makes him a partner is his great project. Interestingly, the initial project is a chimpanzee named Gordon with parts from a variety creatures. After a successful demonstration of the life-giving power of a good electrical jolt, the pair win a sponsor who will allow them to try something much bigger and more human.

The hunchback, who turns out not to be a hunchback, is given the name Igor by his new friend. Igor was Victor's roommate but Victor refuses to elaborate. Hmm. For a maltreated circus clown, Igor is inexplicably brilliant and possess an encyclopedic knowledge of anatomy. He grasps Frankenstein's ideas with ease, though often seeing the trees and ignoring the forest. He also has a better grasp on how to act in polite company than Victor. On top of that, it is implausible for such a gifted medical mind to have been unaware that his affliction was not a hunched back but something entirely treatable.

Victor (James McAvoy) is a true mad scientist. He is full of passion and mood swings. He might be considered manic-depressive, though mostly manic. Wow, really manic. He is impatient with those who cannot grasp his genius. Unrestrained by ethics or morals, he will do whatever it takes to create life. After all, if he can conquer death, will not that outweigh any ill done on the path to achieve it?

Inspector Turpin (Andrew Scott) has an uncanny knack for seeing the truth of things. When first introduced, he demonstrates a keen ability to intuit the truth from the lies that are offered. Though it is never explained why, Turpin is obsessed with a case that involves the theft of animal body parts that have occurred. Though I thought I knew the reason why he was obsessed, it was never confirmed in the movie.

Lorelei (Jessica Brown Findlay), the saved trapeze artist, falls madly in love with Igor. She did the same thing as Sybil in Downtown Abbey, falling for the chauffeur. It is peculiar that Igor the clown - not a lot of skill required - was pursued as he attempted to escape the circus but Lorelei - a major attraction - was abandoned after her injury, not her first. Her happy acquisition of a sugar daddy who has no sexual interest in her is perhaps a bit too convenient. Like Igor, she adapts to polite society with surprising ease.

Of course, it wouldn't be Frankenstein without the monster. The monster does look impressive but doesn't last. Heck, it didn't get out of the castle to wreak havoc on the peasants. Like much of the movie, the creation and destruction of the monster is entirely too convenient. Too much is left nice and tidy. However, Igor does get a letter from Victor in which Victor declares his plan to try again. Was there a plan for a sequel? I rather doubt this will be successful enough to see that happen.

The movie was fun to watch and had a surprising amount of laughs - all provided by Frankenstein, not the clown. Go figure. James McAvoy's wild and frantic Frankenstein was great fun. McAvoy's Frankenstein had more energy than the lightning bolt that gave life to his monster.

Trumbo

We open with some background offered in text. Dalton Trumbo was a member of the Communist Party from 1943 to 1948. In 1947, Trumbo's (Bryan Cranston) career is rocketing, having been signed to the most lucrative contract ever offered to a screenwriter. Then disaster struck as the Congress started looking for communists in Hollywood. Trumbo and others were called to testify but refused to answer the question of 'are you now or have you ever been a communist?' Failure to answer put them in contempt of Congress. Trumbo served 11 months in federal penitentiary after which he was blacklisted.

However, Trumbo continued to make a living as a writer,

passing his work to writers who weren't blacklisted and getting a portion of the pay. He also wrote under several pseudonyms. He is shown assisting his fellow blacklistees to do the same. During this time, two of his screenplays won Oscars.

Hedda Hopper (Helen Mirren) is the big villain and John Wayne (David James Elliot) proves to be a fellow traveler. Ronald Reagan is also shown testifying against Communists before the House Un-American Activities Committee. Hedda is painted as a particularly foul and mean woman, eager to ruin the careers of communists or, in the case of Edward G. Robinson (Michael Stuhlbarg), those who had associated with communists. She, not the government, is the villain in this movie.

One of the funnier moments in the movie was when Trumbo's eldest daughter - about 11 at the time - asked if she was a communist. Trumbo offers a test. He paints a scene where she has a sandwich and some other child does not. What do you do? Tell that child to get a job? Sell the sandwich at a huge profit? "Share," she announced. Yes, you are a communist, her father declares. And that is the limit of the discussion on what communism is.

As far as it goes, the movie tells its story quite well with both humor and drama. The movie shows no doubts about which side is correct and brings up the First Amendment on several occasions. Trumbo comes across as an unflinching defender of freedom of thought. The movie closes with a conciliatory victory speech given in 1970, showing that Trumbo was a bigger, nobler man than one could really expect.

And now the rest of the story...

Almost a decade before the movie begins, Dalton Trumbo wrote an anti-war book called *Johnny Got his Gun*. The book was published only 2 days after World War II commenced. Only the month before that, Russia and Germany had signed the Molotov-Ribbentrop Pact, a non-aggression treaty that preceded the two powers dividing Poland between them. Trumbo's book remained in publication *until* the Nazis attacked Russia. Then, both Trumbo and his publisher pulled it. As a Communist, he now wanted the US to get into the war to assist Russia, the only Communist state at that time. In the wake of WWII, the Iron Curtain brought about many more Communist states in Eastern Europe, all puppets of the growing Soviet Empire. In 1949, China fell to the Communist Mao Zedong. The Fascists - Germany and Italy - at their peak were geographically tiny compared to what the Communists now held.

In WWII, the US *liberated* France, Belgium, Netherlands, et al. Russia *subjugated* Eastern Europe. Trumbo was on the Communists' side! There was no First Amendment protection in the Soviet bloc but Trumbo was eager to use it to allow him to propagandize for the Communists here. His Capitalist counterpart in the Soviet Union ended up in the gulag but the United States is the bad guy. Right.

Communism - as practiced - was the deadliest ideology of the 20th Century. It was far deadlier than Fascism and Nazism combined. Stalin, Mao Zedong, Pol Pot, and their ilk murdered tens of millions. To lionize a communist propagandist just shows that most people are still unaware - by design - just how bad communism was and is.

But back to Trumbo. The Blacklist was not some government requirement that such people not be employed. It was Hollywood itself choosing not to associate with communists. Freedom of association is also in the First Amendment. Trumbo brought his troubles on himself and got off fairly easily.

Tuesday, December 1, 2015

Dump Amnesty to Defeat Trump

Why Doesn't the GOP Elite Give Up on Amnesty?

If the Republican establishment is so panicked about Donald Trump

— a wild, proto-fascist egomaniac with his finger on the button, in their telling — you'd think it would do the one thing that would almost certainly stop him: Surrender. By "surrender" I mean abandon their decades long dream of winning Latino votes through a magic pill called "comprehensive immigration reform" (known to its opponents as amnesty).

...

Is there any doubt that if "comprehensive immigration reform" went away for good, Trumpism would wither? So why don't Haley Barbour and Karl Rove call a big K Street meeting where they say, "Boys, we have to throw the damn yahoos this bone. We're giving up on amnesty"?[48]

Kaus is really onto something here. Why, when the base of the party is clearly attracted to Trump because of his stand on illegal immigration, doesn't the party just adopt that view. This is what your voters want. They want it so much that they will vote for Trump. Trump! Trump is looking more and more like the eventual nominee because the voters don't trust insiders. The party can't wait to try amnesty yet again in spite of their voters.

I don't think the party has time to reverse this problem. With JEB's campaign barely limping along and Rubio under the stain of his Gang of 8 foolishness, there isn't a credible candidate who can seize the anti-amnesty flag from Trump. The most likely candidate with elective experience who could steal the mantle is Ted Cruz, and the party leaders hate him far more than they hate Trump.

Friday, December 4, 2015

President Broken Record

I say this every time we've got one of these mass shootings. This just doesn't happen in other countries,
Barack Obama after San Bernardino Shooting

So quickly we forget Paris, Mr. President? On a per capita basis, there are half a dozen European countries where the odds of getting killed in a mass shooting are higher than in the US. Of course, a mass shooting in Europe has to be much bigger to get any coverage here in the US. Four people killed in Serbia is hardly going to play on the evening news but that same thing in Chattanooga, TN, can run for days. The bias of the news to report US shootings rather than similar shootings in Europe gives verisimilitude to the president's claim. No, the only European shootings reported here are the big ones, like Paris last month, or the massacre of 77 Norwegians - mostly teenagers - in 2011.

As with every such incident, President Obama suggests gun control. It is irrelevant to him that the guns used in the San Bernardino shooting were illegal in California. California has been ratcheting up gun control for years, for the safety of its citizens, don't you know. What gun control does, as I have mentioned time and again, is to disarm the law-abiding while providing a safer environment for the criminals. Criminals hate when their victims shoot back.

Every time Obama broaches the gun control issue, gun sales go through the roof. EVERY TIME. He is a gun store's best advertisement. He must know this. No one has done more for gun proliferation in the past 7 years than Barack Obama. If he had been a gun advocate instead, he would not have been able to convince so many to buy guns. When it is counterproductive to even mention a policy, maybe that is a policy best avoided.

Ideological State of Iraq and Syria

Syed Farook was born in Illinois to Pakistani immigrants. He had worked at the San Bernardino public health department for 5 years. Two years ago, he married his wife, Tashfeen Malik, and they had a baby girl 6 months ago. Then, out of the blue, he and his wife shot more than 30 people, mostly Farook's co-workers. Sure, they were both Muslims but that had nothing to do with it. No, this was probably workplace violence. Oh, the wife pledged allegiance to ISIS on Facebook during the attack? But it still has nothing to do with Islam. Islam is a religion of peace. ISIS, Al-Qaeda, Boko Haram, Hezbollah, Al-Shabaab, Ansar al-Islam, and all the rest are doing Islam wrong.

It turns out that ISIS is not Islamic. Which must mean that all of those other groups aren't Islamic either. There is an interesting article on Think Progress that explains it:

Why ISIS Is Not, In Fact, Islamic

Conservatives reacted harshly to President Obama's claim on Wednesday night that the Islamic State in Iraq and Greater Syria (ISIS) "is not Islamic," accusing the commander-in-chief of naiveté and ignorance. "What kindergartner briefs the President on terrorism?" Ron Christie, a GOP strategist tweeted. "ISIS says it's Islamic, lots of people say it's Islamic, only the president won't," George Will told Fox News shortly after the speech.

But the full context of Obama's remark points to an important distinction between Islam and the extremist ideology that's sweeping parts of Iraq and Syria. "No religion condones the killing of innocents, and the vast majority of ISIL's victims have been Muslim," Obama said. "ISIL is a terrorist organization, pure and simple. And it has no vision other than the slaughter of all who stand in its way."[49]

Well, that cleared things up. So Mohammad wasn't a Muslim. You see, he was a warlord who led his 'peaceful' followers into a score of battles. His followers began as bandits who struck Meccan caravans, the better to get wealth and power. After a successful battle against a Meccan force where he was vastly outnumbered, his following grew. Eventually, he conquered Mecca and then Arabia. It was all done very peacefully because Islam is the religion of peace.

But back to Farook. Though he has been described as 'very religious,' we know that his path led him not to true Islam but to Ideology! Yes, it was an evil Ideology that somehow exclusively afflicts Muslims. Those terror groups have all wrongly appropriated the title of Islam. Of course, no one should ask why Muslims are so susceptible to Ideology. Just be satisfied that Ideology is not Islam. There is *no* link. If you think otherwise, you are an Islamophobe and may be subject to prosecution by the DOJ!

Loretta Lynch Vows to Prosecute Those Who Use 'Anti-Muslim' Speech That 'Edges Toward Violence'

The day after a horrific shooting spree by what appears to be a radicalized Muslim man and his partner in San Bernardino, California, Attorney General Loretta Lynch pledged to a Muslim advocacy and lobbying group that she would take aggressive action against anyone who used "anti-Muslim rhetoric" that "edges toward violence."

Speaking to the audience at the Muslim Advocates' 10th anniversary dinner Thursday, Lynch said her "greatest fear" is the "incredibly disturbing rise of anti-Muslim rhetoric" in America and vowed to prosecute any guilty of what she deemed violence-inspiring speech.[50]

Maybe Attorney General Lynch could use that same reasoning to protect Christians and Jews? Maybe?

Sunday, December 6, 2015

"Conservative" Billionaires for Hillary

Top Jeb Bush political donor in Miami: I'll vote for Hillary Clinton over Donald Trump

One of Florida's biggest conservative Republican moneymen — and a billionaire backer of Jeb Bush — is so disgusted by Donald Trump's candidacy that if he has to, he'll do the unthinkable:

"If I have a choice — and you can put it in bold — if I have a choice between Trump and Hillary Clinton, I'm choosing Hillary," Miami healthcare magnate Mike Fernandez told the Miami Herald on Friday. "She's the lesser of two evils."[51]

What does this say about JEB? It says that JEB is closer to Hillary than to Trump. It says that JEB supporters can more easily swing over to a leftist Democrat than a non-traditional Republican. Really, both JEB and Hillary are in favor of Amnesty and Common Core. Hillary says that Obama's executive amnesty (lawlessness) didn't go far enough! JEB and Hillary could be running mates, which is why JEB's campaign has floundered.

Fernandez calls Trump the next Hitler or Mussolini. Gee, Republicans aren't used to being called fascists on a regular basis. I can't count the number of times that George W. Bush was compared to Hitler or called a Nazi. Of course, the very ones who hurl the fascism/Nazi label usually demonstrate their ignorance. Mussolini was a Socialist who later combined with Nationalism to create National Socialism. Which party has the Socialists again? Isn't Bernie Sanders a self-declared Socialist? But the Republican is the Fascist. Whatever. But let's look at the evidence so far.

What are Trump's declared policies that are either posted on his website or regularly mentioned in his stump speeches?

US-China Trade Reform: Trump thinks we have a bad deal with China as far as trade goes and wants to dramatically reset the table. He makes a lot of good points and has some prescriptions that I like. Notably, he suggests fixing our debt as a means of closing our trade deficit (there is an economic proof that shows that trade deficits are related to debt). I'm doubtful of regaining lost manufacturing jobs but a stronger stance would be generally beneficial.

Veterans Administration Reform: This was briefly a scandal for the Obama Administration and Bush before him. Trump proposes to fix it but so did the current and previous administration. Will Trump follow through? Government agencies are, by their nature, doomed to inefficiency and waste. Trump may be able to improve it but privatization and reimbursement would probably work better.

Tax Reform: Simplify the tax code. He has proposed 4 brackets and a shift in who pays the burden. He particularly mentioned hedge fund managers. Sounds like he wants to tax Wall Street more. Isn't that was Elizabeth Warren wants? Is she a Nazi? I've reviewed Trump's tax ideas in another post and don't need to retread it here.

Second Amendment Rights: He believes in the 2nd Amendment. Trump has bragged about having a gun and even claims to have a concealed carry license. Hitler was a gun-grabber, the better to oppress the citizens. Who else wants to limit the citizens' access to guns? President Obama! Sounds like Obama and the Democrats are closer to Hitler than Trump is.

Immigration Reform: Here's the big one, the one that launched Trump into the lead that he has held for months. Secure the border and eject those who crossed it illegally. Let's enforce the laws that Congress passed. US Immigration should primarily benefit Americans, not foreigners. Why import cheap labor at the expense of increasing the unemployment rate among inner-city youth? Yep, that sounds like Hitler. OMG, the Horror! The Fascism!

War on Terror: Though not listed among his positions on his website, Trump is very strong on this. He has called for bombing ISIS out of existence and not bringing Muslim refugees into the United States.

All of these are popular overall positions with the American electorate. That's why he is viewed as a Populist. However, none of them are Fascist. You might call his immigration policy Nativist, his trade policy Protectionist, or his Tax Reform a giveaway to the wealthy but none of these policies jibe with Hitler. Anyway, Trump is less of a danger than Obama because Trump actually likes America.

DHS, Terrorist Haven?

72 DHS Employees on Terrorist Watch List

At least 72 employees at the Department of Homeland Security are listed on the U.S. terrorist watch list, according to a Democratic lawmaker.

Rep. Stephen Lynch (D., Mass.) disclosed that a congressional investigation recently found that at least 72 people working at DHS also "were on the terrorist watch list."

"Back in August, we did an investigation—the inspector general did—of the Department of Homeland Security, and they had 72 individuals that were on the terrorist watch list that were actually working at the Department of Homeland Security," Lynch told Boston Public Radio.[52]

This does not inspire confidence in government. The agency created to protect the homeland in the wake of the 9/11 attack has hired people on the watch list. How tough is it for the human resources department at DHS to check applicants against the terrorist watch list? Why didn't the FBI give them a heads up?

FBI: Hey DHS, we were checking out someone on the terrorist watch list and discovered he was working as a screener at TSA. What's up with that?

DHS: What? Again? I'll have a chat with Muhammad down in HR.

FBI: Yeah, about Muhammad in HR...

The Department of Homeland Security comprises Transportation Security Administration (TSA), Immigration and Customs Enforcement (ICE), Citizenship and Immigration Services, and the US Border Patrol. These agencies are responsible for keeping the wrong people out of the country or off our airplanes. And they have failed to keep the wrong people out of the department! If 72 people on the terrorist watch list infiltrated the department, how many sneaked by Border Patrol, snookered ICE, or slipped past TSA?

Of course, it is possible in a department of 240,000 people that 72 of them shared names with known terrorists. But if it was just mistaken identity, why did the inspector general report it and Representative Stephen Lynch (D. Mass.) make an issue of it?

Mass Shootings double Under Obama

I stumbled upon a fascinating spreadsheet compiled by Mother Jones.

US Mass Shootings, 1982–2022: Data From Mother Jones' Investigation

The full data set from our in-depth investigation into mass shootings.

This database originally covered cases from 1982 to 2012 and has since been updated and expanded numerous times. For analysis and context on this data—including how we built the database, and a change to the baseline for victim fatalities with cases dating from January 2013—see our Guide to Mass Shootings in America, which includes an interactive map documenting all of the cases.[53]

Obviously, I am not a regular reader of Mother Jones but I must commend it for the logical and complete data that has been compiled. As most of my co-workers know, there are few things that I like more than an Excel spreadsheet. Data in a spreadsheet can reveal a great deal if pressed into a pivot table or sorted by one factor rather than another. There is the opportunity to get subtotals for certain factors and then compare that to subtotals from another factor.

Mother Jones counts 73 mass shootings since 1982, slapping down the Washington Post's claim that San Bernardino was the 355th mass shooting just *this year*. Of course, one must define the terms. Mother Jones only included those incidents where 4 or more were killed and it wasn't gang or drug-related (i.e. the victims had no reason to expect they were at risk of being killed). In those 73 mass shootings, 595 people were killed and 543 were injured. The state with the most mass shootings is California (12), followed by Florida and Washington (6 each), then Texas (5). When looking at the shooters, 43 of them showed prior signs of mental illness. Those 43 shooters accounted for 63% of the fatalities and 71% of the injured. In fact, the mentally ill had a higher average number killed (8.7 victims per shooting) than those who were not mentally ill (7.1 victims).

Now let's drift into unfair and unreasonable territory. Yes, let's ask what portion of the carnage has happened since Hope and Change entered the White House. It turns out that more than a third (26) of the mass shootings have occurred since President Obama was inaugurated. There were only 15 mass shootings during the George W Bush administration, 18 during Clinton, and 7 each during Reagan and George Bush. Let's consider fatalities per month. Reagan saw 0.7 mass shooting fatalities per month during his two terms. Bush I had 1.3, Clinton 1.2, Bush II 1.3, and Obama 2.7. Wow! The number of fatalities per month has more than doubled under Obama. If there was this sort of rise with a Republican in the White House, it would be front page news and appearing on every newscast.

Now here is where we head into the tinfoil hat stuff. This increase in frequency of mass shootings during the Obama Administration does - from his repeatedly stated perspective - add weight to the gun control message. Some speculated that Fast and Furious was meant to get guns into the hands of bad actors, increase gun crime along the border, and provide an impetus for gun control. The very idea reminds me of *The Long Kiss Goodnight* (1996) in which a US intelligence agency plots an attack on America to increase next year's funding from Congress. That doesn't really happen, right?

Krampus

This new Christmas movie doesn't really know what it wants to be. It opens with a very negative view of the consumerism of the season, showing shoppers at some Walmart like store stomp an unfortunate greeter underfoot before getting into brawls over who grabbed this or that first. Stuffed animals are ripped asunder and security guards use tasers with glee. With this, we know a dark Christmas is coming.

The story centers on Max and his family. Max is at an age where belief in Santa is unexpected. He is tormented by his cousins for having written a letter to Santa. Feeling embarrassed, he tears it up and tosses it out the window. Moments later, dark clouds arrive and soon a blizzard of epic proportions knocks out the power. Then it gets really weird.

There are times when the movie wants to explain the pathos of each character, playing like some family drama. We learn that Max's parents have been drifting apart, he is no longer as close to his older sister as he once was, his Uncle Howard wanted boys which is why his older daughters dress and act as they do, and so on and so forth. This family background proceeded beyond the introduction phase of the movie, which was awkward. Max's grandmother spoke almost exclusively in German though everyone else spoke to her in English. That was awkward, especially when she explains the plot to everyone in English halfway through the movie. Worse, she initially gets subtitles and then it stops. Actually, I didn't learn German in the first 20 minutes of the movie; why have the subtitles stopped? The movie was sometimes comical, especially with Uncle Howard.

Krampus is a goat-legged fellow who is the evil Santa in Germanic lore. Where Santa gives presents and spreads joy, Krampus punishes the naughty. And it turns out that Krampus has a number of helpers. There are gingerbread men, an evil teddy bear, a voracious jack-in-the-box, an animated robot toy, a bunch of masked elves, and a never-seen beast that burrows under the snow and drags off characters. This vast menagerie of monsters was exasperating. The movie might have been better called *Minions of Krampus.*

For a horror film, it wasn't scary. After all, Krampus is coming for the naughty people and it is hard to feel much sympathy for many of them. Max - the central character - spends much of the film as a bystander while the adults fight off the latest Krampus goon. The movie ends very badly but then there is a twist which doesn't really improve the ending. This was written and directed by the man who penned the disastrous *Superman Returns* (2006). Skip this one.

Monday, December 7, 2015

Extreme Policy!

In the wake of Obama's milquetoast speech that was more concerned with an American backlash against Muslims than with ISIS killing Americans, it is no surprise that Trump offers the other extreme. Where Obama wants to bring in Syrian refugees over the objections of many governors and legislators, Trump wants to shut down *any* Muslim from entering the country. Pick your bad policy. It is only because of Obama's failed foreign policy that Trump is able to get cheers for his proposed policy. Much the same is happening in Europe. The left-leaning parties have been shown to be unserious about the threat posed by Islamic terrorists so the citizens, with no other option, are voting for reactionaries who will bring a whole host of other issues but at least they appear to be serious about the terror threat. Obama's repeated abdication on illegal immigration and Islamic terrorists has made the rise of Trump possible, even inevitable. Given a choice between being flooded with Muslim refugees who may be infiltrated by ISIS operatives or barring all Muslims from the country, what does the rational person choose? One choice is reckless and one is unjust. Pick!

Has Trump gone too far this time? Probably not. Those who

support him are unfazed by his hyperbole. And this sort of hyperbole was recently practiced by the Democrats. In the wake of Dylan Roof killing 9 black churchgoers, there was a push to strip every Confederate symbol from every public place throughout the south. It went so far that reruns of the *Dukes of Hazzard* were pulled from TV Land because the General Lee sported a Confederate Flag on the roof. So, if it is appropriate to attack all things Confederate over Roof, is it not in the same spirit to deny Muslims access to the US in wake of San Bernardino? The extreme on the one invited the extreme on the other.

After the American Revolution, the Founders had such fear of a powerful central government that they created a pathetically weak one under the Articles of Confederation. They soon learned that government needed to be more powerful to keep the peace but still wanted a limited government. This time, having seen both the extremes, they modeled something more toward the middle which proved to be good policy. Perhaps somewhere between Trump's nativism and Obama's borderless world, there is a good policy to be had. Maybe Ted Cruz can offer that policy.

Tuesday, December 8, 2015

The Art of the Haggle

Anyone who has prepared for an interview and received advice from friends and family is familiar with the idea of asking for more salary than required. The employer will offer something less but higher than would have been offered if the 'real' goal salary had been revealed. This is standard negotiation, seen in films and on TV with such regularity that everyone knows that haggling gets a better deal. But what about legislative policy? Are the wildly unlikely proposals of Donald Trump nothing more than an opening bid? He proposed deporting 10 to 20 million illegals in his first year, something that would require a massive effort and considerable cost if done the way government traditionally does such things. With this as President Trump's demand, what would Congress offer to satisfy him and his supporters; newly elected presidents have a lot of political capital to spend. Or, what of his complete shutdown of all Muslim immigration? Again, this is likely just the beginning of a negotiation. Trump may even believe his stance is extreme but if he offers something more reasonable, he might get less than he really wants. Recall, this is a man who wrote *The Art of the Deal* in the 1980s, a book that was a #1 best seller for a year. Rather than being a nativist crackpot, perhaps Trump is bringing his business negotiation skills to politics. He certainly can't negotiate worse deals than the Republicans have over the last 7 years.

Saturday, December 12, 2015

Bernie Sanders: Economic Illiterate

Looking at Bernie Sander's website and his views on Income and Wealth Equality, I discover that his plans didn't survive some back of the envelope math.

Putting at least 13 million Americans to work by investing $1 trillion over five years towards rebuilding our crumbling roads, bridges, railways, airports, public transit systems, ports, dams, wastewater plants, and other infrastructure needs.

Although I thought Obama had already dealt with this with his trillion dollar stimulus - no, wait. He said shovel-ready wasn't as shovel-ready as he thought. Okay, this still needs to get done. That being the case, let's check the numbers. $1 trillion dollars over a five year period will be $200 billion a year. That $200 billion paid out as salary to 13 million (he said "at least" so we'll go with the minimum) would be $15,384.62 each. Wow, that's not much, certainly not enough to raise a family. And this doesn't even account for the materials needed to do all the rebuilding, so that is a *maximum* salary.

Increasing the federal minimum wage from $7.25 to $15 an hour by

2020. In the year 2015, no one who works 40 hours a week should be living in poverty.

$15 per hour would lead to $120 per 8 hour day or $600 per 5 day week. That would amount to $31,200 a year, more than double what he plans to allocate for workers on his infrastructure project. Well, let's look at that number. $15,384.62 a year comes to $295.86 per week and $59.17 per day. That would be $7.40 an hour, just above the current minimum wage. Could that be a coincidence? Extremely unlikely. Of course, if he gets his minimum wage increase, we'll just have to allocate $2 trillion to the 5 year plan. Easy as pie. It will work much better when Bernie spends twice as much as Obama did. Maybe they are finally shovel-ready?

Creating 1 million jobs for disadvantaged young Americans by investing $5.5 billion in a youth jobs program. Today, the youth unemployment rate is off the charts. We have got to end this tragedy by making sure teenagers and young adults have the jobs they need to move up the economic ladder.

They may be disadvantaged youth but they require the new minimum wage too, right? Therefore, that $5.5 billion divide equally (Bernie is big on income equality) among the million youths would be $5,500 each. At $15 per hour, that is 366 hours and 40 minutes of work or about 9 weeks of full time employment. Is this a summer jobs program? If it is meant to be year round, it will be 7 hours a week. If not, these disadvantaged youth will be unemployed for 43 weeks of the year.

Requiring employers to provide at least 12 weeks of paid family and medical leave; two weeks of paid vacation; and 7 days of paid sick days. Real family values are about making sure that parents have the time they need to bond with their babies and take care of their children and relatives when they get ill.

That sounds very compassionate but increases the cost of labor. How? Let's break it down. Looking at my minimum wage employee who is paid $31,200 a year, even if he and all his family is perfectly healthy, I am only getting $30,000 of labor, the other $1,200 going to his *paid* vacation. Since I don't get those 80 hours of labor, I have to amortize that over the rest of the year. It works out that I am really paying $15.60 per hour. What if he takes all 7 *paid* sick days? Now he is costing me $16.05 per hour. Gads, what if he is out for the 12 week *paid* family medical leave too? Now he is costing $21.31 per hour. Sure, that is the worst case scenario but any woman in her childbearing years will use most or all of her 12 weeks.

With this huge and continuous shift of costs onto employers, is it any wonder that manufacturing is moving overseas? As the cost of labor domestically rises relative to foreign labor, the issue becomes the cost of shipping. With the proliferation of free trade agreements that erase tariffs, that cost is dropping. Voila, China becomes the new manufacturing hub of the world, increased shipping costs are more than offset by the reduction in labor costs, and corporate profits skyrocket. Corporations can move. They will only stay while it is profitable to do so. Bernie's prescriptions will accelerate the exodus. Oh, but Bernie thought of that.

Reversing trade policies like NAFTA, CAFTA, and PNTR with China that have driven down wages and caused the loss of millions of jobs. If corporate America wants us to buy their products they need to manufacture those products in this country, not in China or other low-wage countries.

Not only is Bernie going to more than double the minimum wage, he's going to engage in protectionism. The Smoot-Hawley Tariff Act of 1930 was supposed to get Americans to buy domestically manufactured goods and spur growth after the 1929 market crash. Instead, it cut imports and exports by half through a trade war. Didn't do the Great Depression a bit of good. But maybe it will work for Bernie. The World Trade Organization - of which we are a member - is going to love that.

Ignoring all that, let's just ponder where this goes. The price of all goods in the US is currently based upon the importation of a large percentage of our manufactured goods. Merely undoing that will cause the price of goods to rise dramatically as US labor costs are already higher than overseas. Add to this the greatly increased labor costs. To make up for this upheaval, corporations are going to have to raise prices dramatically. And though government will have been the architect of the disaster, business will be blamed for gouging and being greedy, just like is happening with Obamacare now.

At the end of Bernie's proposed path is an economy worse than what currently exists, perhaps a great deal worse.

Macbeth

A generally faithful retelling of Shakespeare's famous tragedy. Scotland is in a civil war, King Duncan (David Thewlis) against Thane Macdonwald. Macbeth (Michael Fassbender), Thane of Glamis, is Duncan's leading general. Their forces clash in a bloody and gory battle where Macbeth slays the rebel thane but finds that his only remaining son died during the battle. In the aftermath of this battle, he encounters the witches who foretell that he will be Thane of Cawdor and then rise to kingship. He dismisses them but, when he is granted Cawdor by King Duncan, he is set on a dark path. His wife (Marion Cotillard) embraces the idea of kingship and pushes her hesitant husband to slay Duncan. Long a loyal and honorable warrior, Macbeth's sanity cracks in the days and weeks after his foul deed.

The story is powerful and there are lots of opportunities for action but the movie somehow runs at a snail's pace. The overwhelming score is all whole notes that only increase the feeling of slow and ponderous motion, even during battle scenes. However, the breakdown of both Macbeth and Lady Macbeth is done quite well. Macbeth's fracturing sanity soon spreads to his wife. Her pleasure at their new status is quickly destroyed as she sees what a monster her husband has become.

No reason to see this on the big screen. Wait for cable.

How you speak makes a BIG difference

Just watched a clip of Donald Trump in which he was dubbed by someone with a British accent. It is amazing how much more erudite Trump sounds with a British accent. The words are the same but the tone and the delivery are completely different. Here, he doesn't sound brash and arrogant, rather he comes across as a snarky professorial type. It is interesting how an accent can dramatically change how words are interpreted.

Star Wars: The Force Awakens

The movie is good but unfocused and repetitive. Our story opens on the desert planet of Jakku where Poe Dameron is acquiring a map that will allow the Resistance to locate Luke Skywalker, last of the Jedi. Just like Leia in the original movie, Poe's location is attacked and he must hide the map in a droid before he is captured. The droid then falls into the hands of a young woman named Rey. *The Force Awakens* could as easily have been named *A Newer Hope*. Yes, it has an amazing number of similarities to the first movie. Here is a description I found on the Star Wars message board of IMDB:

A rag-tag group of heroes on a desert planet finds a droid with important information. They smuggle it off-planet to the resistance, who are fighting against the imperials. During the climax, they have to rescue the female of the group, disable the shield generator, and destroy the weak spot of the imperial's super weapon, which has the power to destroy planets. During the climax, the old mentor of the group is tragically cut down by the main villain, an evil force user. Despite this, the resistance manages to destroy the super-weapon and temporarily defeat the imperial army.

Yeah, lots of similarities. Our group on the desert planet is Rey and Finn. Rey is shown to have been left – for reasons unknown – on Jakku as a child. She lives in the ruins of an imperial walker and makes a living by scavenging parts from a crashed imperial cruiser. She rescues a droid from another scavenger. Finn the former Stormtrooper arrives on scene and joins her. The two then flee as the First Order seeks to recover the droid. They steal a ship that Rey judges to be garbage; it's the Millennium Falcon. No sooner have they evaded the First Order and gotten into orbit when the ship is caught in a tractor beam and taken aboard an unknown ship.

Enter Han and Chewy. Han offers a brief explanation of how the Falcon was stolen and it has taken this long to track it down. Of course, we have hardly made introductions than Han's bigger ship – which is never named – is boarded by two sets of criminals looking to collect money from Han. This actually bothered me. Han comes across as a newbie smuggler looking for the big score rather than a seasoned veteran who doesn't make such rookie mistakes. In the original trilogy, Han had to dump Jabba's cargo before his ship was boarded. He was competent but he got unlucky. Here, with his weakly comic fast-talking to the two sets of criminals, he comes across as incompetent. This is not the right way for Han to be comic relief. This is a very mellow and dispirited Han Solo. That is explained with later reveals but he felt a shadow of his former self. His death is telegraphed long before it occurs, which drained a lot of the tension. By the time he walks out onto the bridge, it is anticlimactic. I think I would have preferred the fiery old Han lecturing his son about being a damned fool to follow that old fossil Snoke and Ben suddenly snapping and killing him. Anyway, it is widely known that Harrison Ford wanted to be killed off during the original trilogy so his wish finally being granted here is even less of a surprise.

Rey grows in the force at an alarming rate. We first saw hints of her force ability when she flew the Falcon. Then, she really came to life when she resisted Kylo Ren's interrogation. Though he has had training, he soon finds that Rey turns the tables and reads his mind! He has hardly left the cell when she mind controlled a Stormtrooper (played by Daniel "James Bond" Craig) into releasing her. Soon thereafter, she stomps an admittedly wounded Kylo in a lightsaber duel. Heck, she is already well beyond where Luke was at the beginning of Empire Strikes Back and he had had some instruction from a Jedi Master. Obviously, she is the character that the title references but it did seem that her advancement in the force came entirely too quickly and easily.

Fin is an oddity that wasn't explained. Is he the only Stormtrooper to ever balk from butchery? What makes him different? If he has been 'conditioned' since childhood, why is he so normal around non-conditioned people? Are all Stormtroopers this affable once you take off the armor? Also, I found it irritating that the enemy didn't just shoot him. During the fight at the ruins of Maz Kanata's, he is called a traitor and then attacked. Okay, so that Stormtrooper recognizes him. Why not just shoot him? It isn't as if Fin could have blocked blaster fire with the lightsaber. No, the Stormtrooper converted his weapon into some sort of energy club that could block a lightsaber. If you are the kind of guy who guns down unarmed villagers, why aren't you the kind of guy who guns down traitors? Obviously because that would have killed off Fin. Screenwriters need to stop rescuing important characters by having villains act stupidly.

Poe, who is the first hero we meet, vanishes for much of the film. When he is brought back, he takes the role of lead pilot. It isn't Star Wars unless you have some exciting space battles and our other characters aren't yet suited for that. So in comes Poe and his squadron of x-wings. He is pretty exclusively a pilot in the movie.

Kylo Ren is initially very intimidating but, as we get to know him, proves to be a conflicted and moody villain. His tantrums are hilarious. Where his grandfather would Force choke underlings to death to release stress, Kylo hacks inanimate objects to shreds with his lightsaber. In the wake of his betrayal of the Jedi, he is used to being the only person who can use the Force but he has a rude awakening when he squares off with Rey. His lightsaber with its almost flame-like blade strikes me as another sign that he is still unskilled. The blade is unstable which, though scary, also implies that he didn't put it together quite right. Though a lot of grief is being heaped on the character, I liked him. He is what Anakin should have been in the prequel trilogy: very conflicted, at times menacing, at times vulnerable. Anakin was just one long woe-is-me it's not fair the Jedi are evil whine. Piling the chemistry-free love interest with Padme only made it worse. So, Kylo is a vast improvement and I expect he will mature into a more Vader-like villain by the next movie. Killing his father puts him solidly on the Dark Side of the Force and should purge his conflicted feelings.

General Hux is an arrogant and surprisingly young leader. I was initially surprised at how he spoke down to Kylo Ren but that only further demonstrated that Kylo wasn't a Vader clone. Where Grand Moff Tarkin insouciantly stayed on the Death Star despite being told "there is a danger," Hux was the first to evacuate Starkiller Base. Wow, these are some villains. The First Order is proving to be a pale imitation of the Empire.

Captain Phasma decided to shut down the shield because a traitor – who had recently demonstrated that he couldn't shoot unarmed villagers - held a gun to her head. The fate of Starkiller Base is sealed by her decision. Phasma is shown to be a sad excuse for a Stormtrooper and utterly undeserving of her conspicuously shiny armor. Doubtless, she will return but her character has been damaged.

What is the political situation thirty years after the deaths of the Emperor and Darth Vader? General Leia appears to command a single base with a few dozen X-wings. She is part of The Resistance. Resistance to what? The Empire is gone, right? There is a New Republic. We saw the capitol planet of the New Republic destroyed, right? Why aren't Leia, Akbar, and all the rest part of the military of this New Republic? Where are the capital ships aligned with the Republic or the Resistance? The planet where Leia is based is going to be destroyed and the best she can muster is a couple of dozen fighters? Wow, that's pathetic. It very much seems like the First Order is the governing body though, at the same time, they are talking about conquest. But there is virtually nothing standing in your way? Why did you bother with the planet killer if there isn't anyone actually opposing you?

The First Order comes across as generally incompetent. Not one but two of our heroes escape in separate incidents. During one of those escapes, another team has simultaneously infiltrated the base. Their impressive Starkiller Base, like previous planet vaporizing weapons, manages to take one shot before it is destroyed by a handful of enemies. The First Order has great set designers but they aren't so great at the fighting. Of the many battles that First Order fought, they only won one, which was when they attacked a mostly unarmed village. Not an auspicious beginning for the forces of darkness.

There is a new and bigger death star. Wow, we haven't gone there before. Granted, that first one was really quite cool. It was unfortunate that it was destroyed before it got to really instill terror across the galaxy. The second one was pathetic and a death trap. It blew up ships here and there but never got to target a planet. This new one is stupid. I can accept a moon-sized space station with a cannon that is powerful enough to destroy a planet. Hey, it's just physics. A big enough gun will turn a planet into an asteroid field. But Starkiller Base is different. First, it is in System A while the target planet is in System X. The 'projectile' is fired and traverses who knows how many light years in mere moments. Moreover, the projectile – which appears as just an energy beam – has a guidance system that allows it to turn toward the target planet. Maybe that was gravity pulling it to the targets? No, at the speed it was going, a black hole would have trouble modifying its trajectory. I would have gone for a massive torpedo. Yeah, that would be doable. Modify some obsolete frigate, fill it with explosives, and have it hit a planet at light speed. The Starkiller just defied physics. Worse, there was that stupid visual of the planets exploding. If a planet around Alpha Centauri exploded, we wouldn't know about it on Earth for years. And we certainly wouldn't be able to see the explosion during daylight with the naked eye! Even though this is science-fantasy, this really grated on me. Much as I think it has been done quite enough, I would have preferred Death Star 3 to this travesty.

This far, far away galaxy has never heard of a history book. In the first trilogy, characters have never heard of the Jedi and find the Force to be something bizarre. But in the prequels, the Jedi Council is a branch of galactic governance, its members are the generals during the Clone Wars. Heck, Chewy fought alongside Yoda! Now in this one, Rey thinks Luke Skywalker is a myth! That Han has to confirm Luke's existence is just odd. "The Berlin Wall, the Cold War. It's all true." Even in the prequels, this problem persisted. In such a technologically advanced society, how did a whole star system just vanish from the star charts and only some short order cook knew about it?

Speaking of star charts, what was with that kooky map? In the super high-tech world of Star Wars, there is no such thing as email. The map is on a memory chip of some kind and can never be copied or transmitted. Moreover, shouldn't it just be galactic coordinates. I'm sure there must be some mapping system similar to latitude and longitude that would map even unexplored regions. Even when the data is at the Resistance base in the dormant R2-D2, it is inaccessible. How does technology work in this galaxy? Of course, this could now be a complaint of the original movie. Why didn't Leia just email the Death Star plans to the Rebel Alliance? Email was virtually unknown in 1977. In 2015, we can watch a movie on a phone that fits in our pocket. It is troubling that some of our current technology exceeds that of the Star Wars universe.

Luke does not appear until the final scene. He was kept out of the story because including him would have undercut the new characters. Really, once Luke is on scene, he becomes the central character while everyone else is a sidekick. Though I understand the reasoning, it makes Luke look bad. One of his apprentices has just turned to the Dark Side and killed the other Jedi trainees so Luke runs away and hides? Moreover, he left some sort of map to find him. Are we playing hide and seek? It is going to take some good writing to rehabilitate Luke from this apparently cowardly act.

The most important thing about *The Force Awakens* is the absence of a Jar Jar Binks character. Nor was there any mention of midi-chlorians. And, as already mentioned, the central character wasn't a plaintive Anakin. Yes, it is a rehash, it has lots of unanswered questions, it used some weak plot devices, but it was fun. Most of the characters have lots of promise for future development.

Friday, December 25, 2015

Pirate Latitudes

This posthumously published Michael Crichton book seems very unlike his other work. It is a straightforward pirate adventure tale and does not seem interested in instructing the reader. I've read a fair number of his books and his villains are typically shallow and underdeveloped, his heroes are often similarly two-dimensional, but his storylines are often complex but rarely fully developed. Most of that is true here as well. It is possible that, were I not already quite familiar with the region and the period, the book would seem more educational. He does touch on a lot of facets of the period in a fairly short novel. Where *Timeline* and *Sphere* felt like science lectures, *Pirate Latitudes* was more of a refresher.

The story opens at the governor's mansion in Port Royal, Jamaica. Governor Almont has a busy day ahead of him. In a chance conversation, he learns of a Spanish treasure ship that did not make the voyage across the Atlantic with the rest of the Spanish fleet. Opportunity! At this point, the story shifts to Captain Charles Hunter, a privateer on good terms with the governor. Hunter goes in search of the perfect crew to accomplish an impossible task. It seems rather like the *Dirty Dozen* which then transitions to the *Guns of Navarone*. Oddly, getting the treasure is not the finish. No, now it becomes *The Odyssey* as Hunter must return to Port Royal, overcoming treachery, a hurricane, a pursuing Spanish galleon, and cannibals.

Though sometimes outlandish, it is a fun read.

The Expanse

This new *Syfy* series takes place in the 23rd century, after humanity has managed to colonize the moon, Mars, various outer planetary moons, and the asteroid belt. The story opens with a woman stuck in a cell in a weightless environment. She manages to breakout and explore. When she sees something inexplicable, she screams!

The story resumes on Ceres, a dwarf planet in the asteroid belt, where Detective Joe Miller is given an off-the-books assignment to find a missing rich girl, none other than the woman in the opening scene. Elsewhere, the ice hauler Canterbury is returning to Ceres from Saturn where it collected giant blocks of ice from the rings. They receive a distress call, which they initially ignore but later investigate. A team of 5 take a shuttle to board the stricken ship. It proves to be a trap!

Solar politics is a big theme in the series, mostly explored through Chrisjen Avasarala, a UN bigwig who has no qualms about being ruthless despite her apparently affable facade. The UN governs all the moons and outposts through the solar system except for Mars, which is independent. There is a movement among the 'Belters' to likewise become independent. Belters appear to be anyone who is neither an Earther nor a Martian, the largest population of them being on Ceres. The Outer Planets Alliance (OPA) - a group that claims to represent the Belters - is generally viewed as a terrorist organization. There is a lot of tension between Earth and Mars as well.

The setting feels very real. The technology doesn't seem quite advanced enough but still beyond what currently exists. Ships have gravity by accelerating, not by some magical artificial gravity machine; there are times when characters are weightless. It felt a lot like *2001: A Space Odyssey* without the psychedelic light show at the end.

If the first 4 episodes are indicative of the first season, this is going to be an awesome show. Highly recommended, so far.

Sunday, December 27, 2015

The Big Short

A quirky documentary-like dramedy about the housing collapse of 2007. The story follows several characters who learn of the weakness of the various mortgage-based bonds and seek to profit on their inevitable collapse. It starts with Michael Burry (Christian Bale), an MD who runs a hedge fund. He is the first to see weakness in the subprime mortgage market and invests the majority of his fund in credit default swaps. As such, he was betting that the subprime market would crash. Per the film, his purchases attracted the interest of other investors, first Jared Vennett (Ryan Gosling). Vennett sold credit default swaps to FrontPoint Partners, run by Mark Baum (Steve Carell). There are also a couple of young men with dreams of grandeur who happen upon a Vennett prospectus concerning the coming subprime meltdown. With the help of a former banker (Brad Pitt), the two also manage to acquire credit default swaps. When the collapse comes, all of them become rich while the economy nose dives.

Mark Baum is perhaps the best character from the viewer's perspective because he expresses the outrage that many viewers likely feel. While the other characters are out to profit, he is the one trying to uncover how deep the rot goes. He is the one who finds that Standard & Poor's offers AAA ratings to crap bonds because, if not, Moody's will; why drive business to the competitor? Realtors are selling houses with no regard to credit because the mortgage is just going to get bundled with countless other mortgages. The home buyers are buying because the houses appreciate so much that they earn rapid equity, can quickly refinance, and draw money out! He later discovers that a $50 million collateralized debt obligation (CDO) – which is a bundling of all these mortgages – could have as much as $1 billion associated with it through even more technical and abstruse financial instruments. The rot goes to the bone. He concludes that the banks knew the subprime market was a time bomb but didn't care because the government would bail them out. Taxpayers, not the banks, paid for the banks' reckless, even fraudulent, behavior.

The movie has a vibe to it like *The Office* (2005-2013). Characters, even minor ones, will turn to the camera and offer asides, sometimes explaining that it didn't actually happen as shown. The breaking of the fourth wall is most common for Vennett, who serves as a narrator for the backstory and offers pithy commentary through the film. Then we have random cameos by Selena Gomez and Margot Robbie to explain arcane financial concepts in a way that retains the viewers' attention. Clever but again a fourth wall breach. The movie comes across as an effort to educate in an entertaining way.

I enjoyed the film but it gives a one-sided view of the crash, blaming the banks and Wall Street but generally giving a pass to the government. Sure, there is an SEC regulator who is actively seeking a job at one of the big banks and it is clear that whatever agency is meant to keep the banks in line is asleep at the wheel. What isn't brought up is the Community Reinvestment Act or the threats by Janet Reno of potential action against banks if 'redlining' didn't stop. There was no talk of Bush's Ownership Society. The Feds spent the previous 10 to 15 years demanding that banks loosen the requirements for home loans or else. Or else what? No law was passed but the banks got the message. Banks made it easier to get a loan. These eased requirements, which provided loans to people less likely or able to pay them, are the basis for blaming the 'poor and immigrants.' The movie does mention the accusation but doesn't provide the background to the claim. Hmm.

Though I clearly learned some things about the subprime meltdown that I didn't know, it didn't cover some things that I did know. Take it as a primer but not as a conclusion. The story is more complicated still. Check out this Podcast (https://www.econtalk.org/roberts-on-the-crisis/) from Russ Roberts about the financial crisis.

Thursday, December 31, 2015

The Four Stages of Jihad

AnsweringMuslims.com is a website that examines the documentary evidence found in the Koran and other Islamic writings. One video[54] was particularly informative. Citing the Koran extensively, there are several stages of jihad. Interestingly, they coincide very much with Mohammed's life and can also be seen throughout the world today.

Stage 1: Stealth Jihad

This describes Muslims who are in an area completely dominated by peoples of other faiths. Open jihad would result in total defeat and is thus counterproductive. In this stage, the Muslim must present themselves as friendly and deserving of respect. State a willingness to live and let live and explain how Islam is a religion of peace. This is the stage where many American-based Muslims find themselves. This stage correlates to Mohammed's time in Mecca when he began preaching.

Stage 2: Defensive Jihad

Once the Muslim community is sufficiently protected, the level of intolerance for critics of Islam rises. Speaking ill of Islam can provoke assassinations and terrorism. Many places in Africa, Asia, and even Europe are at this stage. This stage correlates to Mohammed's time in Medina when he practiced banditry against Meccan caravans and killed or expelled critics of himself or Islam.

Stage 3: Offensive Jihad

The Muslim community is now the majority. Non-Muslims must convert, pay a tax to practice their religion, or be slaughtered. No churches or synagogues may be constructed within Muslim-controlled territory. Conquest is desirable, if possible. Saudi Arabia, Iran, and the Islamic State are at this stage. This correlates with Mohammed's conquest of Mecca and then the rest of Arabia.

Stage 0: Clueless about Jihad

These Muslims are mostly cultural Muslims who have not read the Koran and are thus largely unaware of what it commands. These people are similar to many Americans, who are culturally Christian - this includes the new pagans and atheists - but not actively attending church and only have a vague notion of what's in the Bible. There is also a large chunk of the American Jewish community that is culturally and ethnically Jewish rather than religiously Jewish.

There is an obvious bias but David Wood has clearly read the source material. He makes an excellent argument and the stages fit nicely with the world as we find it. Moreover, it fits with my knowledge of history and follows closely with Mohammed's life. The three stages of Jihad are practically a biography of Mohammed. The video is just under half an hour but most enlightening.

The Lost Future

The story opens with a band of Stone Age hunters trekking through the forest in search of prey. At one point, the eldest of the hunters calls for a halt, stating they have reached the edge of their territory. Savan insists on going further. The band comes upon a giant sloth, which they kill. While celebrating their success, one of their number stumbles among them with a nasty bite to his arm. In moments, his appearance changes and he begs his comrades to kill him.

On the way back to the village, they are watched by an archer (Sean Bean). As they enter the village, the archer pulls out a pair of binoculars! Yes, it turns out that this is the Post-Apocalypse and a plague has turned much of humanity into zombie-like creatures. The town elders are furious that the hunters went beyond the normal boundaries and are soon proven correct. Insane mutant humans descend upon the village. Many escape to hide in a barricaded cave. Savan, Dorel, and Kaleb escape into the woods.

Savan is a brash youth, in line to be a chief, and the default leader of the trio. He is the slowest to accept new things, like boats, bows, or venturing beyond the homeland. However, he is brave, daring, and ready to sacrifice himself for the good of others. Dorel is his mate, a gorgeous blonde in a leather bikini. Kaleb is the outcast, son of a crazy man who had ventured into the wilds many times before finally vanishing for good. Kaleb is also the last literate person. The trio soon meet Amal, the archer who has been watching. Amal knew Kaleb's father and tells a tale of the downfall of civilization centuries ago. Amal further explains that Kaleb's father had found a cure for the plague but Gagen stole it for himself and his tribe. With no hope of rescuing those stuck in the cave without help, the little band set out to recruit those who aided Kaleb's father and take back the cure that Gagen stole.

The movie is often clunky and very uneven. That Kaleb is literate – thanks to his father – but none of his father's former associates is literate doesn't make sense. However, it makes Kaleb indispensable for deciphering his father's work and perhaps making more of the cure. Right, so when the plague was ravaging the world, the best medical labs couldn't develop a cure but, in the Stone Age technology long afterward, one man was able to concoct something that is both a cure and a vaccine against future infection. Call me a skeptic. Also, why didn't his father introduce the bow to his tribe while he was teaching his son to read?

When Amal signals for reinforcements, half a dozen men arrive on horseback, a band of horse archers. So, Gagen stole the cure from these guys? Fine. Meanwhile, Savan, Dorel, and Kaleb go to Gagen's island and manage to abscond with the cure. These three mostly clueless kids accomplished what Amal and his allies could not? When Gagen chases after the cure, the most precious thing he owns, he takes three men with him. On foot, no less! That's it? That's all you are willing to commit to recovering the cure? How did he steal it again? Imagine if Gagen and his party stumbled on Amal and the horse archers; he'd be toast.

In the climactic battle where Amal and his band are slaughtering the mutant humans who are loitering around Kaleb's village, Gagen arrives. He is alone. His crossbow has one shot. He shoots at Kaleb, the only person with any hope of recreating the cure. Genius!

The idea of the movie was interesting, kind of like *I Am Legend*, only a couple centuries later. The execution was lacking. However, the most interesting thing about the movie is that Sean Bean does *not* die (check out this video <https://

www.youtube.com/watch?v=WZfPaePwiI4> that shows why his survival is worth mentioning). Though it looked like he might be done a couple of times, he pulled through to the finish. Way to go, Sean!

Not worth watching unless, like me, you are a Sean Bean fan. I've been a fan since I first saw him in *Sharpe's Rifles* and all the Sharpe's movies that followed. To me, that is his signature role though Boromir comes in as a close second.

---

[1] http://newsbusters.org/blogs/mike-ciandella/2014/01/02/frozen-out-98-stories-ignore-ice-bound-ship-was-global-warming-missi

[2] http://www.usatoday.com/story/weather/2013/12/31/record-cold-temperatures/4264237/

[3] http://www.telegraph.co.uk/news/worldnews/northamerica/usa/10581947/The-real-life-Wolf-of-Wall-Street-behind-the-Scorsese-film.html

[4] https://www.breitbart.com/politics/2014/03/23/no-justice-department-charges-against-ohio-woman-who-voted-six-times-for-obama/

[5] http://reason.com/blog/2014/06/20/the-irs-had-a-contract-with-an-email-bac

[6] https://www.telegraph.co.uk/news/earth/environment/10916086/The-scandal-of-fiddled-global-warming-data.html

[7] https://www.teapartypatriots.org/about/

[8] https://www.theguardian.com/world/2014/sep/20/polygamist-women-utah-sex-assault-case?CMP=twt_gu

[9] https://www.telegraph.co.uk/news/worldnews/islamic-state/11156264/Iraq-asks-for-US-ground-troops-as-Isil-threaten-Baghdad.html

[10] https://legalinsurrection.com/2014/11/completely-clueless-week-at-college-insurrection/?utm_source=feedburner&utm_medium=feed&utm_campaign=Feed%3A+LegalInsurrection+%28Le%C2%B7gal+In%C2%B7sur%C2%B7rec%C2%B7tion%29

[11] https://www.mediaite.com/tv/obamacare-architect-lack-of-transparency-helped-us-pass-the-law/

[12] https://www.nytimes.com/2014/11/23/world/middleeast/

thousands-of-iraq-chemical-weapons-destroyed-in-open-air-watchdog-says-.html?mabReward=RI%3A7&action=click&contentCollection=Energy%20%26%20Environment%20®ion=Footer&module=Recommendation&src=recg&pgtype=article&_r=0

[13] https://www.telegraph.co.uk/news/earth/environment/globalwarming/11395516/The-fiddling-with-temperature-data-is-the-biggest-science-scandal-ever.html

[14] https://www.washingtontimes.com/news/2015/feb/26/irs-watchdog-reveals-lois-lerner-missing-emails-no/

[15] https://www.dailymail.co.uk/sciencetech/article-3156594/Is-mini-ICE-AGE-way-Scientists-warn-sun-sleep-2020-cause-temperatures-plummet.html

[16] https://www.ctpost.com/news/article/Democrats-drop-Thomas-Jefferson-and-Andrew-6400544.php

[17] https://claremontreviewofbooks.com/the-politics-of-star-trek/

[18] https://www.latimes.com/science/sciencenow/la-sci-sn-science-quiz-americans-pew-20150909-story.html

[19] https://therightscoop.com/democrat-mutiny-dnc-chair-debbie-schultz-heckled-by-huge-crowd/

[20] https://www.5newsonline.com/article/news/local/outreach/back-to-school/woman-desperate-to-be-blind-had-drain-cleaner-poured-in-eyes-now-happier-than-ever/527-856a2f12-6b55-411b-8c2a-8aecd376a57d

[21] https://www.nytimes.com/2015/08/24/world/middleeast/in-pushing-for-the-iran-nuclear-deal-obamas-rationale-shows-flaws.html?_r=0

[22] http://www.foxnews.com/world/2015/09/03/iran-thumbs-nose-at-us-even-as-obama-rallies-support-for-nuke-deal/?intcmp=hpbt1

[23] http://www.reuters.com/article/2015/09/10/us-mideast-crisis-syria-exclusive-idUSKCN0R91H720150910

[24] https://www.politico.com/story/2015/09/iran-deal-senate-dems-block-gop-measure-to-kill-213506

[25] https://www.defenseone.com/threats/2015/09/nato-caught-surprised-russias-move-syria/120764/

[26] https://ca.news.yahoo.com/iran-says-finds-unexpectedly-high-uranium-104622948.html

[27] https://news.yahoo.com/russia-positioning-tanks-syria-airfield-u-officials-144236303.html

[28] https://freebeacon.com/national-security/obama-admin-iranian-ballistic-missile-tests-not-a-nuke-deal-violation/

[29] https://www.wsj.com/articles/u-s-defense-secretary-discusses-syria-with-russian-counterpart-1442589965

[30] https://www.wsj.com/articles/russia-expands-military-its-presence-in-syria-satellite-photos-show-1442937150

[31] https://news.yahoo.com/russia-iran-throw-weight-behind-assad-un-meet-210506731.html

[32] https://freebeacon.com/national-security/iran-buys-21-billion-in-aircraft-satellites-from-russia/

[33] https://web.archive.org/web/20151005063942/http://www.reuters.com:80/article/2015/10/01/us-mideast-crisis-syria-iranians-idUSKCN0RV4DN20151001?

[34] https://www.nytimes.com/2015/10/01/world/europe/russia-airstrikes-syria.html

[35] https://www.bloomberg.com/opinion/articles/2015-10-02/putin-has-his-own-no-fly-zone-in-syria

[36] https://www.nytimes.com/2015/10/05/world/middleeast/us-aims-to-put-more-pressure-on-isis-in-syria.html?src=twr&_r=0

[37] https://www.nytimes.com/2015/10/05/world/middleeast/us-aims-to-put-more-pressure-on-isis-in-syria.html?src=twr&_r=0

[38] https://www.washingtonpost.com/world/syrian-activists-russian-air-strikes-pound-rebel-zones-in-latest-blows/2015/10/07/fb3be168-5cf3-4e38-98f3-f6b75ed53871_story.html

[39] http://www.foxnews.com/politics/2015/10/09/exclusive-us-officials-conclude-iran-deal-violates-federal-law/

[40] https://www.nytimes.com/2015/10/10/world/middleeast/pentagon-program-islamic-state-syria.html

[41] https://www.dailymail.co.uk/sciencetech/article-3291456/Monkeys-heading-MARS-Russian-scientists-training-macaques-solve-puzzles-travel-space-2017.html

[42] https://cnsnews.com/news/article/penny-starr/atheist-okay-disparage-christians-islam-limits-because-fear

[43] http://usuncut.com/world/france-24-blasts-republicans-blaming-attacks/

[44] https://news.yahoo.com/two-men-linked-paris-attacks-registered-migrants-greece-195255102.html

[45] https://www.breitbart.com/politics/2015/11/18/report-8-syrians-caught-at-texas-border-in-laredo/

[46] https://dailycaller.com/2015/11/18/princeton-students-take-

over-presidents-office-demand-erasure-of-woodrow-wilson/

[47] https://www.theguardian.com/world/2015/oct/06/nato-chief-jens-stoltenberg-russia-turkish-airspace-violations-syria

[48] http://www.kausfiles.com/2015/11/30/why-doesnt-the-gop-elite-give-up-on-amnesty/

[49] https://archive.thinkprogress.org/why-isis-is-not-in-fact-islamic-de0219ee3a11/

[50] https://www.dailywire.com/news/loretta-lynch-vows-prosecute-those-who-use-anti-james-barrett

[51] http://www.miamiherald.com/news/politics-government/elections-2016/article48067815.html

[52] https://freebeacon.com/national-security/72-dhs-employees-on-terrorist-watch-list/

[53] https://www.motherjones.com/politics/2012/12/mass-shootings-mother-jones-full-data/

[54] https://www.youtube.com/watch?v=UPLqVL4GHVU

www.ingramcontent.com/pod-product-compliance
Lightning Source LLC
Chambersburg PA
CBHW071222260726

48653CB00042B/1538